Have You Received the

HOLY SPIRIT

Since You

Believed?

BOBBY COLEMAN

Have You Received the Holy Spirit Since You Believed?

Contents

Foreword

The ministry of the Holy Spirit is one of the most profound, yet often misunderstood, overlooked or under-appreciated aspects of the Christian faith. For many believers, the Holy Spirit is merely an abstract concept or an occasional influence, rather than the powerful, personal, and present Helper that Jesus promised. Yet Scripture reveals that the Holy Spirit is essential to our walk with God—He is our guide, our comforter, our teacher, and the very source of power for victorious Christian living.

In *Have You Received the Holy Spirit Since You Believed?*, Bobby unveils the truth about the twofold work of the Holy Spirit—His indwelling presence at salvation and His infilling power for service. Drawing deeply from Scripture, this book lays a solid foundation for understanding that receiving the Holy Spirit is not merely a one-time event, but an ongoing relationship that empowers believers to live as witnesses for Jesus Christ.

As you read, you will discover the powerful truth that salvation is the starting point—not the finish line—in your walk with God. Much like moving into a new home, salvation marks the beginning, but the fullness of the Spirit equips and empowers you to thrive. Jesus Himself illustrated this truth through His teaching, describing salvation as a *fountain of living water* springing up to eternal life and the infilling of the Spirit as *rivers of living water* flowing out to touch and transform the world.

The stories of the early church, from Pentecost to Philip's ministry in Samaria and Paul's encounter on the road to Damascus, show us a clear pattern: believers first received salvation and then experienced a subsequent infilling of the Holy Spirit's power. This truth is not just historical—it is vital for every believer today.

In a world filled with uncertainty, darkness, and spiritual opposition, we need the power of the Holy Spirit more than ever. The gifts of the Spirit, which some have wrongly claimed have ceased, are still essential for advancing God's kingdom and overcoming the forces of evil in our generation.

As you read this book, may your heart be stirred to pursue the fullness of the Holy Spirit in your life. May you experience not only the joy of salvation but also the empowerment that comes from being filled with the Spirit—a life marked by boldness, power, and supernatural impact.

Prepare to be challenged, inspired, and equipped to walk in the power that Jesus promised. The Holy Spirit is not distant or disconnected—He is present, powerful, and available to you today. As you open these pages, open your heart to the fullness of what He desires to do in and through you.

Caleb Ring

Senior Pastor
River Clermont

Introduction

For many in the church today, Holy Spirit is an enigma. The word *enigma* is defined as a person or thing that is mysterious, puzzling, or difficult to understand, yet this is not at all what God intended for believers. There are several reasons for this, the most obvious being that we have an enemy, the deceiver and accuser of our souls, who certainly uses the lack of knowledge to keep believers weak, fearful, and frustrated.

In the Old Testament, the prophet Hosea prophesied a strong rebuke to the nation of Israel, God's covenant nation, which certainly still applies to us today as believers who are to be a holy priesthood unto God.

> My people are destroyed for lack of knowledge (Hosea 4:6a AMPC).

We have an enemy in this life who wants to kill, steal, and destroy everything in our lives that remotely resembles God or His character. This is very evident in today's culture that has embraced immorality and wickedness at a level we've never seen or experienced in the past.

However, I have very good news for you! When we live baptized in the Holy Spirit and fire, every (not some) plan of the enemy is burned up in that fire, and revival breaks out with mighty signs and wonders. This was supposed to be normal for the children of God; Holy Spirit was sent to be our Helper and to lead us in our daily lives as a powerful inner witness. The believer who burns white hot for God in the power of the Holy Spirit will remain strong and do great exploits.

> Those who do wickedly against the covenant he shall corrupt with flattery; but the people who know their God shall be strong, and carry out great exploits (Daniel 11:32).

The word *exploits* means to make full use of and to maximize the benefits of a resource, and that resource for us is the Holy Spirit. God the Father expects us to make full use of Holy Spirit's power, wisdom, peace, and abilities today just like in the days of old. Jesus promised that God the Father would send one just like Himself to be our Helper to lead us in all truth, and that we would receive power when the Holy Spirit comes upon us.

> But you shall receive power when the Holy Spirit has come upon you; and you shall be witnesses to Me in Jerusalem, and in all Judea and Samaria, and to the end of the earth (Acts 1:8).

Introduction

Nothing on the earth has more power or authority than the Holy Spirit, and He works that power through believers. Just like when Jesus walked among us, Holy Spirit is the dominant spiritual force in the world today, and He dwells among us and in us. This is why we cannot be ignorant or allow ourselves to be disarmed of all God promised us when Jesus promised to ask the Father to give us another Helper.

> If you love Me, keep My commandments. And I will pray the Father, and He will give you another Helper, that He may abide with you forever—the Spirit of truth, whom the world cannot receive, because it neither sees Him nor knows Him; but you know Him, for He dwells with you and will be in you. I will not leave you orphans; I will come to you. (John 14:15-18).

Don't miss what Jesus said in this passage, for it is the whole reason for this book: Holy Spirit dwells with us and will be in us! Understanding this passage and all it means to a believer is how we have power to operate in this life the same way Jesus did during His earthly ministry when He was anointed with the same Holy Spirit and power.

> Most assuredly, I say to you, he who believes in Me, the works that I do he will do also; and greater works than these he will do, because I go to My Father. And whatever you ask in My name, that I will do, that the Father may

be glorified in the Son. If you ask anything in
My name, I will do it (John 14:12-14).

This powerful truth "greater works than these will
you do" is how we live this life from victory to victory; it's how we can boldly proclaim that God is still
the healer, the deliverer, the reconciler, the provider, and
soon coming King. The key to victory and those greater
works is to do what Jesus instructed us to do: ask. Jesus'
half-brother James understood this simple, yet profound
key when he said in James 4:2 that we don't have what
we want because we don't ask God for it.

It's time for us to make a demand in faith on the God
of miracles who answers through the power of the Holy
Spirit who lives inside of us. By faith, we will co-labor
with the Holy Spirit, our Helper, and receive all that Jesus
commanded every believer to receive. Let's get after it!

Chapter 1: Have You Received Since You Believed?

He said unto them, Have ye received the Holy Ghost since ye believed? And they said unto him, We have not so much as heard whether there be any Holy Ghost (Acts 19:2 KJV).

Holy Spirit is not an "it" or some mystical force; He is a person, the third person of the Trinity. God is a Triune God—Father, Son, and Holy Spirit. Unfortunately, Holy Spirit is the least understood member of the Trinity, and because of this, many are weak and underequipped for life's struggles. It is imperative that we understand the ministry of the Holy Spirit, how He is our Helper, and how His ministry glorifies the Lord Jesus.

As a born-again believer there is nothing more important in your Christian walk than having a personal relationship with the Holy Spirit. Through salvation we received forgiveness and were reconciled back to God through the blood of Jesus. Now, as Jesus commanded, it is our responsibility and great blessing to work out our salvation through the power of the Holy Spirit who dwells in us.

Many who confess to believe in the Holy Spirit get off to a poor start because of what they are taught, so let's start with what happens when a person is born again. Many denominational churches teach that at salvation when Holy Spirit comes to live in you there is nothing more for you to receive. Although it is true that when someone is born again Holy Spirit indwells their spirit, it could not be further from the truth that there is nothing more for you to receive from Holy Spirit.

Salvation in Jesus' name is not the end-all for a believer, but only the beginning. During His earthly ministry, Jesus taught specifically about the twofold work of Holy Spirit—first an *indwelling,* and afterward an *infilling.* Holy Spirit first indwells the born-again believer and imparts His divine nature in them through the fruit of the Spirit, and then He infills and empowers believers for service through the gifts of the Spirit.

> But the **Helper, the Holy Spirit**, whom the Father will send in My name, He will teach you all things, and bring to your remembrance all things that I said to you (John 14:26).

Think of it like this: your born-again spirit is like buying a house; it's your house but you don't sleep on the floor in your house, you get yourself a bed and you sleep on a bed. In your house you have a stove, but if you want to make breakfast you don't crack an egg right onto the burner, you get yourself pots and pans and cook your eggs in a pan on your stove. When you need to go to work you don't sit down in your driveway or on your garage floor and hope you'll get to work, you get yourself a vehicle and drive yourself to work.

I oversimplified this, of course, but you get the point. Just having a house is not all there is to making it a home. It's the same with the Spirit of God who said He would make His home in us. Becoming born again isn't just about avoiding hell, but for advancing the kingdom of God through works of faith and enjoying the blessings of eternity right here and now.

Two Works of the Holy Spirit: Indwelling and Infilling

During His earthly ministry, Jesus used water to symbolize this twofold work of the Holy Spirit. When He and His disciples were traveling to Galilee from Judea, they stopped to rest in the Samaritan village of Sychar, which is where Jesus encountered the woman at the well and taught her that salvation is like a well of living water bubbling up from within.

> Jesus answered and said to her, "Whoever drinks of this water will thirst again, but whoever drinks of the water that I shall give

15

> him will never thirst. But the water that I
> shall give him will become in him a fountain
> of water springing up into everlasting life"
> (John 4:13-14).

Jesus referred to everlasting life as a fountain of water. The Amplified Version of this verse refers to salvation as "a spring continually flowing and bubbling within."

A short time later on the last day of the Feast of Tabernacles, Jesus used water again to symbolize a subsequent work of Holy Spirit.

> On the last day, that great day of the feast,
> Jesus stood and cried out, saying, "If anyone
> thirsts, let him come to Me and drink. He who
> believes in Me, as the Scripture has said, out of
> his heart will flow rivers of living water." **But
> this He spoke concerning the Spirit, whom
> those believing in Him would receive; for
> the Holy Spirit was not yet given, because
> Jesus was not yet glorified** (John 7:37-39).

This was a direct reference to the infilling of the Holy Spirit and His power, which is a *separate* work after the indwelling of the Holy Spirit at salvation. Jesus taught that the newly born-again believer has a fountain bubbling up to everlasting life, and then Holy Spirit causes rivers of living water to flow out of the believers so that they can be His witnesses.

The disciples were born again when Jesus breathed on them and said "receive the Holy Spirit" on the night of His resurrection.

> That Sunday evening the disciples were meeting behind locked doors because they were afraid of the Jewish leaders. Suddenly, Jesus was standing there among them! "Peace be with you," he said. As he spoke, he showed them the wounds in his hands and his side. They were filled with joy when they saw the Lord! Again he said, "Peace be with you. As the Father has sent me, so I am sending you." **Then he breathed on them and said, "Receive the Holy Spirit"** (John 20:19-22 NLT).

When Jesus breathed on the disciples and said, "Receive the Holy Spirit," this was part of mankind's restoration back to how it was in the beginning when God first breathed His life into man in the garden.

> And the LORD God formed man of the dust of the ground, and breathed into his nostrils the breath of life; and man became a living being (Genesis 2:7).

When God breathed the breath of life into man, he became a living being: a spirit man who has a soul and lives in a body. Afterward, when man sinned and his spirit suffered spiritual death, God promised to redeem mankind and restore His indwelling presence back into the spirit of man. As Jesus breathed on His disciples and said, "receive the Holy Spirit," God was making good on His promise—mankind could now be born again by the recreative power of the Holy Spirit.

After salvation, the infilling of the Holy Spirit is a separate, subsequent work of the Holy Spirit. As Jesus spoke with His disciples before His ascension, He was instructing them to be prepared to receive the infilling or the deposit of God's power into their born again spirit.

At the end of the book of Luke and also at the start of the book of Acts (both written by Luke), Jesus told His disciples, who had already received salvation and were born again, to wait in Jerusalem till "I send the promise of My Father upon you." The purpose of the promise was so that after they were baptized in the Holy Spirit they would be endued with power to be His witnesses from Jerusalem to the ends of the earth.

> Then He said to them, "Thus it is written, and thus it was necessary for the Christ to suffer and to rise from the dead the third day, and that repentance and remission of sins should be preached in His name to all nations, beginning at Jerusalem. And you are witnesses of these things. **Behold, I send the Promise of My Father upon you; but tarry in the city of Jerusalem until you are endued with power from on high**" (Luke 24:46-49).

And being assembled together with them, He commanded them not to depart from Jerusalem, **but to wait for the Promise of the Father**, "which," He said, **"you have heard from Me; for John truly baptized with water, but you shall be baptized with the Holy Spirit not many days from now...**But **you shall receive power when the Holy Spirit has come upon you;** and you shall be witnesses to Me in Jerusalem, and in all Judea and Samaria, and to the end of the earth" (Acts 1:4-5, 8).

The First Baptism of Fire

Ten days after Jesus was carried into heaven (which was fifty days after His resurrection) we find ourselves at the day of Pentecost.

When the Day of Pentecost had fully come, they were all with one accord in one place. And suddenly there came a sound from heaven, as of a rushing mighty wind, and it filled the whole house where they were sitting. **Then there appeared to them divided tongues, as of fire, and one sat upon each of them. And they were all filled with the Holy Spirit and began to speak with other tongues**, as the Spirit gave them utterance (Acts 2:1-4).

As the believers were gathered together, the Holy Spirit filled all who were in the house, and they all began to speak in tongues. This is exactly what John the Baptist said would happen through Jesus' ministry.

> John answered, saying to all, "I indeed baptize you with water; but One mightier than I is coming, whose sandal strap I am not worthy to loose. **He will baptize you with the Holy Spirit and fire** (Luke 3:16).

The Holy Spirit infills believers with His gifts and power to do great works of service still today just as He did on the day of Pentecost. This process can only happen in the life of a born-again believer because the Spirit of truth cannot be received by the world, so until a person is born again, they cannot even receive the Holy Spirit.

> And I will pray the Father, and He will give you another Helper, that He may abide with you forever—**the Spirit of truth, whom the world cannot receive**, because it neither sees Him nor knows Him; but you know Him, for He dwells with you and will be in you (John 14:16-17).

The baptism in the Holy Spirit on the day of Pentecost set the believers into a new dispensation, "the church age," which we are still living in until Christ's return. Unfortunately, some denominations are in great error because they believe and teach that the gifts of the

Spirit have ceased and are no longer in operation today. I respectfully ask you, especially in the world we live in today, do you really believe we no longer need the power of the Holy Spirit to overcome all that hell has unleashed on this world in these last days?

As the commotion of all that took place that morning in the upper room made its way out into the streets of Jerusalem, many were confused and amazed at all they had just seen and heard. Peter, who just weeks before during the mock trial and crucifixion of Jesus denied he even knew the Lord, was now empowered by Holy Spirit to boldly preach his first Spirit-filled sermon.

> Then Peter said to them, "Repent, and let every one of you be baptized in the name of Jesus Christ for the remission of sins; and you shall receive the gift of the Holy Spirit. **For the promise is to you and to your children, and to all who are afar off, as many as the Lord our God will call**" (Acts 2:38-39).

As long as God is still calling the lost to repent through salvation, and He is, then God is still pouring out the promise of the Holy Spirit because He said it was for all who were afar off, as many as the Lord our God will call—and that includes me, you, and our children too.

This is the firsthand account of the apostles, who received straight from the Lord what would happen. We see this pattern repeated multiple times in the early church and in the lives of many believers throughout the book of Acts. So we see there are two distinct works of the Holy Spirit: first an indwelling at salvation and then an infilling with the power to be a witness with signs and wonders following the believer.

Jesus promised we would receive power to be His witnesses to the uttermost parts of the earth, yet many denominational churches who profess to believe in salvation find it hard to reach the lost with the message of salvation. Why is this? Because they do not teach that the Holy Spirit is still filling believers through the gifts of the Spirit.

Before his powerful encounter with the Lord Jesus and the Holy Spirit, Paul (whose name was Saul back then) was actually persecuting believers and was directly involved in stoning Stephen (one of the early church's first deacons) to death for preaching that Jesus was the Messiah. Because of the intense persecution unleashed on the believers in Jerusalem, they began to disperse and to preach the gospel in every town and village they entered, just as Jesus had instructed.

One of the first seven deacons of the church was Phillip (see Acts 7:5-6). We know from Scripture that he was full of faith and the Holy Spirit, and when he left Jerusalem he began to preach the gospel in every village he entered. Later, Phillip would come to be known as Phillip the Evangelist, but here in Samaria, he was just another believer sharing his faith and preaching the gospel with signs and wonders as he flowed in the gifts of the Spirit.

> Then Philip went down to the city of Samaria and preached Christ to them. And the multitudes with one accord heeded the things spoken by Philip, hearing and seeing the miracles which he did. For unclean spirits, crying with a loud voice, came out of many who were possessed; and many who were paralyzed and lame were healed. And there was great joy in that city (Acts 8:5-8).

> Now when the apostles who were at Jerusalem heard that Samaria had **received the word of God**, they sent Peter and John to them, who, when they had come down, **prayed for them that they might receive the Holy Spirit**. For as yet He had fallen upon none of them. **They had only been baptized in the name of the Lord Jesus. Then they laid hands on them, and they received the Holy Spirit** (Acts 8:14-17).

There are two distinct works of the Holy Spirit listed here. First, the people of Samaria received the word of God and were baptized in the name of Jesus. Then after they were saved, Peter and John came down and laid hands on them to receive the Holy Spirit. The Samaritans became born again when they received the word of

23

God (indwelling), and then they received power (infilling) when Peter and John laid hands on them to receive the Holy Spirit.

First, they received the word. Jesus is the Word (see John 1:1). Then they received the Holy Spirit. The Holy Spirit recreates man's spirit and indwells the new believer when they receive Jesus as Lord. Then He infills believers when they receive His power like at Pentecost.

This same thing happened to Saul as he was on his way to persecute and imprison the believers in Damascus. As he was on his way, suddenly a light shone on him from heaven and Jesus spoke to him.

> Then he fell to the ground, and heard a voice saying to him, "Saul, Saul, why are you persecuting Me?" And he said, "Who are You, Lord?" Then the Lord said, "I am Jesus, whom you are persecuting. It is hard for you to kick against the goads." So he, trembling and astonished, said, "Lord, what do You want me to do?" Then the Lord said to him, "**Arise and go into the city, and you will be told what you must do**" (Acts 9:4-6).

When the encounter was over, he had been physically blinded, and the men who were with him led him into Damascus, where he stayed for three days and nights, unable to see and without food or drink. On the third day, a believer named Ananias was sent to Paul so he could receive his sight and be filled with the Holy Spirit.

> And Ananias went his way and entered the house; and laying his hands on him he said, **"Brother Saul, the Lord Jesus, who appeared to you on the road as you came, has sent me that you may receive your sight and be filled with the Holy Spirit**." Immediately there fell from his eyes something like scales, and he received his sight at once; and he arose and was baptized (Acts 9:17-18).

In that first encounter, Saul called Jesus "Lord." Saul received salvation when he called Jesus Lord and obeyed His instructions. Then when Ananias arrived, he acknowledged Saul as a brother in the Lord. Afterward, when Ananias laid hands on Paul just as the Lord instructed, Paul was filled with the Holy Spirit.

Paul received according to the same pattern as the believers in Samaria and the same pattern Paul himself followed later when he was preaching in Ephesus.

> And it happened, while Apollos was at Corinth, that Paul, having passed through the upper regions, came to Ephesus. And finding some disciples he said to them, "Did you receive the Holy Spirit when you believed?" So they said to him, **"We have not so much as heard whether there is a Holy Spirit**." And he said

to them, **"Into what then were you baptized?"** So they said, "Into John's baptism."
Then Paul said, "John indeed baptized with
a baptism of repentance, saying to the people
that they should believe on Him who would
come after him, that is, on Christ Jesus." When
they heard this, they were baptized in the
name of the Lord Jesus. **And when Paul had
laid hands on them, the Holy Spirit came
upon them, and they spoke with tongues
and prophesied** (Acts 19:1-6).

Paul made sure the believers in Ephesus were born
again and then laid his hands on them to receive the
baptism of the Holy Spirit. I showed you the entire
Scripture passage for all three of these incidences to
lay the foundation that salvation (indwelling) occurred
first in all these examples and then an empowering
(infilling) occurred afterward. Each of these specific manifestations is ample proof that the believers
received this infilling of the Holy Ghost and they all
spoke in tongues like the disciples did on the day of
Pentecost.

The Apostle Peter experienced this same pattern
also as he preached to Cornelius' household. Cornelius was a Roman army officer who had a visit from
an angel who instructed him to invite Peter to come to
his house. This was significant because as a Gentile,
Cornelius' household would have been considered an
unclean place for Peter to be found. But after the Lord

sent a vision three times to Peter to let him know he should go with the messengers sent by Cornelious, Peter went and became the first to bring the gospel message to the Gentiles. As Peter began to preach about Jesus and they believed that Jesus was the Messiah, the Holy Spirit fell on them and they also began to speak in tongues just like on the day of Pentecost.

> Even as Peter was saying these things, the **Holy Spirit fell upon all who were listening to the message**. The Jewish believers who came with Peter were amazed that the gift of the Holy Spirit had been poured out on the Gentiles, too. **For they heard them speaking in other tongues and praising God** (Acts 10:44-45 NLT).

This same biblical pattern is found throughout the book of Acts—first salvation by receiving the Word of God and then being baptized in the Holy Spirit with the evidence of speaking in tongues. We see it in the upper room, in Samaria and Damascus, in Ephesus, and here in Cornelius' household. This pattern was the expectation of the early church—and we have never been told to stop following this pattern.

Just as salvation is not the end-all for the works of Holy Spirit, it is also true that speaking in tongues is not the end-all of the gifts of the Spirit; it is the *initial evidence* or sign that we have been filled.

Speaking in tongues is how we build ourselves up in the spirit, and also how we keep ourselves continually aware of Holy Spirit's presence in our lives. Both of these are keys to manifesting the fruit of the Spirit and operating in the gifts of the Spirit. The Apostle Paul made this very clear in multiple letters to the churches.

> But you, beloved, building yourselves up on your most holy faith, praying in the Holy Spirit (Jude 20).

> For he who speaks in a tongue does not speak to men but to God, for no one understands him; however, in the spirit he speaks mysteries...He who speaks in a tongue edifies himself (1 Corinthians 14:2,4a)

> Likewise the Spirit also helps in our weaknesses. For we do not know what we should pray for as we ought, but the Spirit Himself makes intercession for us with groanings which cannot be uttered. Now He who searches the hearts knows what the mind of the Spirit is, because He makes intercession for the saints according to the will of God (Romans 8:26-27).

The word *uttered* in the original language is more of a phase than a simple word, and is expressed as groanings that are too deep for words in a known language; in other words, the Holy Spirit helps us pray to God in our heavenly language when we don't know how to express in the words of our known language what we need to pray. This is exactly what Holy Spirit has done for me and through me thousands of times in my own personal experience over the last forty-plus years of being a believer.

Praying in tongues is also the source of much confusion because too often folks fail to understand there are two types of praying in tongues and do not make the distinction between the two.

- There are tongues that are for every believer. This is the initial evidence that we have received an infilling like on the day of Pentecost. Every believer should possess a personal prayer language; this is what all the scripture references we just read are pertaining to.

- There is also the gift of tongues as one of the nine gifts of the Spirit, which must be accompanied by the gift of interpretation. We will study on the nine gifts of the Spirit shortly.

As we close this chapter, it is vital to understand that you are a spirit who has a soul and lives in a body. I implore you with great urgency, if you have asked Jesus to be your Lord but you have not yet received the baptism of the Holy Spirit and fire, to ask the Lord to fill you today. Just receive; the gift of God has already been given!

Faith Declaration:

I declare today that I believe in the pattern I see in the book of Acts! I ask You, Holy Spirit, to fill me now with Your power with the evidence of speaking in tongues.

Chapter 2: Holy Spirit Indwells

And I will pray the Father, and He will give you another **Helper**, that **He** may abide with you forever—the Spirit of truth, whom the world cannot receive, because it neither sees **Him** nor knows **Him**; but you know **Him**, for **He dwells with you and will be in you** (John 14:12-17).

U nder the old covenant, Holy Spirit rested on and worked alongside prophets, priests, and kings on behalf of the people. In the new covenant, which is based on better promises, Jesus said, "the Holy Spirit who dwells with you will also be in you." As Jesus spoke with the disciples at the Last Supper, He was instructing them about what would happen after He returned to the Father and how Holy Spirit would come as our Helper to guide us in all truth and tell us of things to come.

But now I go away to Him who sent Me, and none of you asks Me, "Where are You going?"

But because I have said these things to you, sorrow has filled your heart. Nevertheless I tell you the truth. **It is to your advantage that I go away; for if I do not go away, the Helper will not come to you**; but if I depart, I will send Him to you. And when He has come, He will convict the world of sin, and of righteousness, and of judgment: of sin, because they do not believe in Me; of righteousness, because I go to My Father and you see Me no more; of judgment, because the ruler of this world is judged. I still have many things to say to you, but you cannot bear them now. **However, when He, the Spirit of truth, has come, He will guide you into all truth**; for He will not speak on His own authority, but whatever He hears He will speak; and **He will tell you things to come. He will glorify Me, for He will take of what is Mine and declare it to you**. All things that the Father has are Mine. Therefore I said that He will take of Mine and declare it to you (John 16:5-15).

The culmination of Jesus' earthly ministry would now shift from His disciples following Him to preparing His disciples—and later all humanity—to follow Holy Spirit. Jesus said this was to our advantage, but how would that transition occur and how would that be to our advantage?

The morning after His mock trial and the scourging that Jesus suffered for all mankind, we read about His final few moments. As Jesus hung on the cross He said, "I thirst," so they held up a sponge of sour wine to his lips. After He received the sour wine He said, "It is finished." What did Jesus mean? What was finished?

> After this, Jesus, knowing that **all things were now accomplished**, that the Scripture might be fulfilled, said, "**I thirst!**" Now a vessel full of sour wine was sitting there; and they filled a sponge with sour wine, put it on hyssop, and put it to His mouth. So when Jesus had received the sour wine, He said, "**It is finished!**" And bowing His head, He gave up His spirit (John 19:28-30)

The gospel of Matthew brings additional details to what happened in those final moments before Jesus died on the cross.

> And Jesus cried out again with a loud voice, and yielded up His spirit. **Then, behold, the veil of the temple was torn in two from top to bottom**; and the earth quaked, and the rocks were split, and the graves were opened; and many bodies of the saints who had fallen asleep were raised; and coming out of the graves after His resurrection, they went into the holy city and appeared to many. So when the centurion and those with him, who were

guarding Jesus, saw the earthquake and the things that had happened, they feared greatly, saying, "Truly this was the Son of God!" (Matthew 27:50-54)

For context, the veil mentioned in the passage above separated the Holy of Holies, the innermost sacred area of the temple, which contained the Ark of the Covenant and the mercy seat of God, from the rest of the temple. It was approximately 30 feet wide, 30 feet high, and 4 inches thick! Once a year on Yom Kippur, which is the Day of Atonement, the High Priest entered into the Holy of Holies to burn incense and to sprinkle blood on the mercy seat of the Ark. He was required to wash himself and put on special clothing before he entered behind the veil. He carried burning incense with him so the smoke would rise and prevent him from looking directly at God while he brought the sacrificial blood with him to make atonement for the sins of the people. The veil was the separation between God and His holiness and man and his sinfulness. When God ripped the veil in two from top to bottom, the separation between God and man was over.

The very moment Jesus said, "It is finished" and gave up His spirit, the old covenant was finished with all its rituals and sacrifices because Jesus became our once-and-forever lasting sacrifice. Once Jesus rose from the dead and carried His blood into the heavenly Holy of Holies and sprinkled His blood on the mercy seat in heaven, the new covenant was ratified.

> And so, dear brothers and sisters, we can boldly enter heaven's Most Holy Place because of the blood of Jesus. By his death, Jesus opened a new and life-giving way through the curtain into the Most Holy Place (Hebrews 10:19-20 NLT).

The New King James Version says, "By a new and living way which He consecrated for us, through the veil, that is, His flesh." Between these two translations we see that through His death and resurrection, Jesus provided us with a new and living way of access to the Father.

Many may ask, "If Holy Spirit had to depart from Adam when he sinned, why doesn't He have to depart from us when we sin?" When Adam sinned and disobeyed God's command, there was no way to forgive and cleanse that act of sin. The wages of sin is death; sin is a spiritual matter which had to be dealt with in the spirit and required the life blood of Jesus to fully and completely once and forever pay the price of sin. Jesus' blood washed away sin; it did not just cover it as the ritual sacrifices had done.

> But if we walk in the light as He is in the light, we have fellowship with one another, and the **blood of Jesus Christ His Son cleanses us from all sin**. If we say that we have no sin, we deceive ourselves, and the truth is not in us. If we confess our sins, **He is faithful and just to forgive us our sins and to cleanse us from all unrighteousness.** If we say that we

have not sinned, we make Him a liar, and His word is not in us (1 John 1:7-10).

When Jesus celebrated Passover with His disciples and said, "This is My body which is given for you," His eyes were on the veil of separation that would soon be torn apart. Holy Spirit, who had made his home in the Holy of Holies made by the hands of man, would now make His home in the spirit of man just as He did when God breathed the breath of life into Adam.

When the veil was torn, Jesus opened the way for us to receive the indwelling presence of Holy Spirit just like Adam did in the beginning. After His resurrection, Jesus became a life-giving spirit and breathed the Spirit of God back into the fallen spirit of man.

> That Sunday evening the disciples were meeting behind locked doors because they were afraid of the Jewish leaders. Suddenly, Jesus was standing there among them! "Peace be with you," he said. As he spoke, he showed them the wounds in his hands and his side. They were filled with joy when they saw the Lord! Again he said, "Peace be with you. As the Father has sent me, so I am sending you." **Then he breathed on them and said, "Receive the Holy Spirit"** (John 20:19-22 NLT).

When we are born again it is not just an experience, it's far more than that—we actually receive the person of

Holy Spirit into our born-again spirit as we, by faith, confess Jesus as our Lord. We become a recreated spirit being who partakes in the divine nature of God by His design, just like Adam partook of the fallen nature of Satan when he sinned and suffered spiritual death. God imparts His nature back into the spirit of man, and our bodies become the new temple of Holy Spirit. The born-again believer becomes the new Holy of Holies on the earth!

> Or do you not know **that your body is the temple of the Holy Spirit who is in you**, whom you have from God, and you are not your own? For you were bought at a price; therefore glorify God in your body and in your spirit, which are God's (1 Corinthians 6:19-20).

The redemption of man involved the recreation of man's fallen spirit as an inner work within. It's an indwelling of Holy Spirit as we just explained. Then as a separate, distinct work, we receive an infilling or empowering through the baptism of Holy Spirit. These two works also accompany specific manifestations of Holy Spirit in the life of the believer and are clearly demonstrated throughout the book of Acts.

Direct Result of the Holy Spirit Indwelling: The Fruit of the Spirit

There are nine fruits of the Spirit, which are the character and nature of God deposited into every born-again believer when we are indwelled by the Holy Spirit. When we yield to Holy Spirit who now lives in us, the fruit will display the character of God in our new life in Christ. The fruit of the Spirit demonstrate the nature of God working in us, and the nine gifts of the Spirit, which we will study later, demonstrate the power of God working through us.

We will also do an in-depth study on the gifts of the Spirit later on in this book, but right now I want to focus on the fruit of the Spirit. We will talk about the first fruit in this chapter and the other eight in the following chapter.

Galatians 5 gives us a listing of these nine fruits.

> But the Holy Spirit produces this kind of fruit in our lives: love, joy, peace, patience, kindness, goodness, faithfulness, gentleness, and self-control. There is no law against these things! (Galatians 5:22-23 NLT)

The fruit of the Spirit develops the divine nature of God in the born-again believer's life the same way the fallen nature of man develops the works of the flesh (senses) in a person who is not yet born again.

> When you follow the desires of your sinful nature, the results are very clear: sexual immorality, impurity, lustful pleasures, idolatry, sorcery, hostility, quarreling, jealousy, outbursts of anger, selfish ambition, dissension, division,

envy, drunkenness, wild parties, and other sins like these. Let me tell you again, as I have before, that anyone living that sort of life will not inherit the Kingdom of God (Galatians 5:19-21 NLT).

The first thing to understand about these nine fruits of the Spirit is that they are not just behavioral modification traits or characteristics which are contrary to the works of the flesh. The knowledge we function in before we are born again is based on our senses, how we think, how we feel, and what we desire. The Apostle Paul called this living in the flesh. Man's soul (his mind, will, and emotions) began to take the lead after Adam and Eve suffered spiritual death. All who followed after them began to be led by and driven by the fallen sinful nature of Satan, which they inherited after Adam and Eve sinned against God.

> However, you are not [living] in the flesh [controlled by the sinful nature] but in the Spirit, **if in fact the Spirit of God lives in you** [directing and guiding you]. But if anyone does not have the Spirit of Christ, he does not belong to Him [and is not a child of God] (Romans 8:9 AMP).

Once we are born again the new recreated spirit in a person should rule his soul, reigning over how we think and how we feel. Our spiritual order has been reset; man is a spirit who has a soul and lives in a body. We can't manufacture the fruit of the Spirit in our lives by how well we try to behave or perform. The fruits of the Spirit are supernatural manifestations in our lives that go far beyond our human capabilities of how well we manage our flesh. As we now study the fruit of the Spirit, you will begin to see and understand that the motivation that causes them to work and manifest in our lives is love.

The fruits of the Spirit are deposited into our inner man when we become born again, but we must tend to the fruit of the Spirit like Adam and Eve were commissioned to tend to the garden of Eden. As we allow the Spirit to control our thoughts and resulting decisions, we are transformed into the image of Christ. Without the inner working of the Holy Spirit in our newly recreated born-again spirit, we cannot begin to manifest the fruit of the Spirit. As we now study on the fruit of the Spirit you will begin to see and understand the motivation that causes them all to work and manifest in our lives is love.

Love: The First Fruit of the Spirit

It's no mistake that the first fruit of the Spirit listed is love. Everything we do for the kingdom of God should flow out of our love for God and our love for others. In fact, when one of the religious leaders tested Jesus by asking what commandment was the greatest, the Lord stressed that all the written Word of God hung on loving God and loving others (see Matthew 22:34-40). Then when Paul was describing all the manifestation gifts of the Spirit, he went so far as to say you can be raising people from the dead and performing miracles, but if it doesn't flow out of a heart of love, it's worthless.

The English language only has one word for love. However, the Greek language has four—three of which we can produce naturally by how we act or feel, but there is only one form of love that is produced spiritually through the divine nature of God in our lives.

Those four Greek words for love are as *eros*, which refers to physical or sexual love; *philos*, which is a warm affection or friendship love; and within *philos* is a related type of love, *storge'*, which refers to strong devotion or family devotion.

The last Greek word for love is *agape,* which is the divine, sacrificial, unconditional love of God. The agape love of God is the first fruit of the Spirit. It is the type of love Paul describes in 1 Corinthians 13:4, "Love is patient and kind. Love is not jealous or boastful or proud." It was because of God's agape love that He continued to pursue and redeem fallen man. God did not abandon mankind, but rescued us because He created us to be His children.

> See how very much our Father **loves** us, for he calls us his children, and that is what we are! But the people who belong to this world don't recognize that we are God's children because they don't know him (1 John 3:1 NLT).

As Jesus was instructing the disciples at the last supper about the Helper, He used symbolic language that makes perfect sense now that the Holy Spirit is able to dwell in the spirit of man again.

> I am the true grapevine, and my Father is the gardener. He cuts off every branch of mine that doesn't produce fruit, and he prunes the branches that do bear fruit so they will produce even more. You have already been pruned and purified by the message I have given you. Remain in me, and I will remain in you. For a branch cannot produce fruit if it is severed from the vine, and you cannot be fruitful unless you remain in me. Yes, I am the vine; you are the branches. Those who remain in me, and I in them, will produce much fruit. For apart from me you can do nothing (John 15:1-5 NLT).

Natural branches can only produce fruit when they remain connected to the vine. Likewise, the fruit of the Spirit can only be produced in our lives as we remain connected to Christ and allow Holy Spirit to lead and guide us.

Agape love empowers believers to act out of sacrificial and unconditional love. Throughout our lives, there will be many instances when it will be much easier to lash out, take vengeance, gossip, or cut people off, but the agape love flowing first and foremost will help the other fruit manifest consistently in your life.

> But **love your enemies**, do good, and lend, hoping for nothing in return; and your reward will be great, and you will be sons of the Most High. For He is kind to the unthankful and evil (Luke 6:35).

> Now hope does not disappoint, because the **love of God** has been poured out in our hearts by the Holy Spirit who was given to us (Romans 5:5).

I hope you see how important it is to allow the Holy Spirit to manifest agape love—the first fruit of the Spirit—in your life. Let's take a look at the other eight fruits of the Spirit, and you'll see how they all flow out of love.

Faith Declaration:

The veil that separated me from God has been torn apart. I am now able to receive both salvation as an indwelling work of the Holy Spirit, and will live according to the nature of God in me through the fruit of the Spirit.

Chapter 3: The Fruit of the Holy Spirit

> But the Holy Spirit produces this kind of fruit in our lives: love, joy, peace, patience, kindness, goodness, faithfulness, gentleness, and self-control. There is no law against these things! (Galatians 5:22-23 NLT)

Joy: The Second Fruit of the Spirit

The Greek word for the fruit of joy is *chara*, and it means far more than mere happiness. Happiness is based on circumstances and satisfying the senses; happiness is very fragile and easy to spoil. Joy may be the sweetest of the fruits of the Spirit (yes, pun intended) because it is the force behind much of what we are called to do with our new spirit man. Joy is the source of *strength* in a believer.

As Jesus continued His teaching that He is the vine and we are the branches, He said those who remained in Him would produce much fruit. Let's continue reading John 15 and discover the next fruit of the Spirit.

If you keep My commandments, you will abide in **My love**, just as I have kept My Father's commandments and abide in **His love**. "These things I have spoken to you, that **My joy** may remain in you, and *that* **your joy** may be full. This is My commandment, that you love one another as I have loved you (John 15:10-12).

We see two of the fruits here in this passage—the agape love we talked about in the last chapter, and then Jesus makes the distinction between His joy and our joy. He said "when *My* joy remains in you, *your* joy will be full." Later, after their last supper together in the upper room ended, Jesus prayed to the Father for the disciples to experience His joy fully and completely.

But now I am coming to You; and I say these things [while I am still] in the world so that they may experience **My Joy** made full *and* complete *and* perfect within them [filling their hearts with My delight] (John 17:13 AMP).

Joy is the overwhelming response of believers who follow Holy Spirit's guidance and allow Him to be their Helper. This is a choice, not an emotion. However, once they make the choice to follow, there is oftentimes an exuberance that accompanies that choice.

I may not always "feel" like doing certain things that I am led to do, but once I fully engage and choose to follow, it is amazing how often the joy of the Lord manifests in me with great expression. Joy is the spiritual response to salvation, and it is our strength. This kind of joy is what happened after Nehemiah finished rebuilding the walls and gate of Jerusalem that had lain in ruin. Once everything was completed, all the people gathered together for a great celebration and the reading of God's Word, and they became overwhelmed with emotion and wept at God's faithfulness.

> Then Nehemiah the governor, Ezra the priest and scribe, and the Levites who were interpreting for the people said to them, "Don't mourn or weep on such a day as this! For today is a sacred day before the LORD your God." For the people had all been weeping as they listened to the words of the Law. And Nehemiah continued, "Go and celebrate with a feast of rich foods and sweet drinks, and share gifts of food with people who have nothing prepared. This is a sacred day before our Lord. Don't be dejected and sad, for the **joy of the LORD** is your strength!" (Nehemiah 8:9-10 NLT)

Dear friend, the fruit of joy becomes your strength, which empowers you to do all things through Christ, and it will always be the force behind your choice to follow the leading of Holy Spirit.

Peace: The Third Fruit of the Spirit

The Greek word for the fruit of peace is *eirene,* which refers to a state of quietness, rest, repose, harmony, order, and security in the midst of turmoil, strife, and temptation.[1] We live in a world that needs the fruit of peace to manifest in the life of every born-again child of God!

When God blessed Adam and Eve with the creation covenant blessing, part of that four-fold blessing encompassed peace.

> Then God blessed them, and God said to them, "Be fruitful and multiply; fill the earth and **subdue** it; have dominion over the fish of the sea, over the birds of the air, and over every living thing that moves on the earth" (Genesis 1:28).

The word *subdue* means to overcome, quieten, or bring under control. I am sure most of you understand what overcoming means as well as to bring something under control, so I want to expound on the word *quieten*, which is an old English word that refers to an amazing demonstration of peace, to become or make calm and quiet.

Imagine a newborn baby who is fussing, which turns into full-blown crying and agitation. Grandma goes and picks up the baby and tries to calm the child to no avail.

---

1. *Strong's Concordance*, s.v. "eirēnē" (G1515), Blue Letter Bible, accessed February, 18, 2025, https://www.blueletterbible.org/lexicon/g1515/kjv/tr/0-1/.

The father says, "Here, Mom, let me try," again to no avail. The father hands the baby to the mother, and as the mom holds the baby close to her chest and gently rocks the child, she says, "Shh-shh-shh-shh," and the baby quietens. It's a deep peace and calm, a place of familiar security.

This is what God blessed Adam and Eve to do throughout the earth when He instructed them to subdue what He had given them to rule and reign over. The fruit of peace is far more than the absence of difficulties; it is the confident trust we have in the Holy Ghost to lead us, guide us, and help us overcome in any situation. It is to be the one who quietens any circumstance.

> But the **Helper**, the Holy Spirit, whom the Father will send in My name, He will **teach you all things**, and bring to your remembrance all things that I said to you. **Peace I leave with you, My peace I give to you**; not as the world gives do I give to you. Let not your heart be troubled, neither let it be afraid (John 14:26-27).

Learn to yield to Holy Spirit and allow the fruit of peace to manifest in your life.

Patience/Long-suffering: The Fourth Fruit of the Spirit

The fruit of patience is also known as long-suffering. The Greek word *makrothumia* is patient endurance;

consistency, steadfastness, perseverance; slowness in avenging wrongs.[2]

This is where I found my own biggest struggle. Bearing the offenses and provocations of others without murmuring certainly has to be divine because this is one of the easiest areas to react according to one's thoughts, emotions, and feelings. Where many miss this (and I certainly did and do) is in our first reaction. When an offense comes, the first response to any provocation, offense, or especially false accusation can either shut the thing down or empower it in our lives.

Not many find it easy to patiently endure being provoked or offended, especially without just cause. This is still a place where I must strongly yield to Holy Spirit, but I have found strength to overcome (or at least do a serious attitude check), after I realize my emotions are trying to take control, by yielding to Holy Spirit and quieting my own soul. If you find yourself doing the same thing at times, read these words of Jesus who taught on this very subject.

> Love your enemies! Do good to them. Lend
> to them without expecting to be repaid. Then
> your reward from heaven will be very great,
> and you will truly be acting as children of
> the Most High, **for he is kind to those who**

2. *Strong's Concordance*, s.v. "makrothymia" (G3115), Blue Letter Bible, accessed February 18, 2025, https://www.blueletterbible.org/lexicon/g3115/kjv/tr/0-1/.

are unthankful and wicked. You must be compassionate, just as your Father is compassionate. "Do not judge others, and you will not be judged. Do not condemn others, or it will all come back against you. Forgive others, and you will be forgiven. Give, and you will receive. Your gift will return to you in full—pressed down, shaken together to make room for more, running over, and poured into your lap. The amount you give will determine the amount you get back" (Luke 6:35-38 NLT).

Long-suffering is how God has been and continues to be with mankind, and He has called us to be like-minded toward one another. When we yield to the fruit of patience in our lives and do not allow our emotions to react first when offended or challenged, we have this promise—when patience has its perfect work in us, we will be perfected (mature) and complete, lacking nothing.

My brethren, count it all joy when you fall into various trials, knowing that the testing of your faith produces patience. **But let patience have its perfect work, that you may be perfect and complete, lacking nothing**. If any of you lacks wisdom, let him ask of God, who gives to all liberally and without reproach, and it will be given to him (James 1:2-5).

Kindness: The Fifth Fruit of the Spirit

The fruit of kindness is the Greek word *chrestotes*, which refers to a disposition to be gentle, soft-spoken, kind, even tempered, cultured, and refined in character and conduct. In our harsh world, gentleness is often misinterpreted as weakness or considered to be a trait of those who are naïve or get taken advantage of. But this is not how the Lord sees this fruit.

God says kindness is a strength that few are willing to allow to work through them in these last days, when the love of many has grown cold. But we are a chosen generation, a holy people who love the Lord.

> Since God chose you to be the holy people he loves, you must clothe yourselves with tenderhearted mercy, **kindness**, humility, **gentleness**, and patience (Colossians 3:12 NLT).

The divine nature of God's kindness and gentleness is demonstrated in how we treat others, especially when they cannot repay or return that act of kindness back to us. In this way, we show that the love of God and the fruit of kindness has overtaken our old selfish nature, and we are no longer living to please ourselves but rather God.

As I was praying about the fruit of kindness, the Lord reminded me of a particular act of kindness that Lisa and I have both done several times over the years, which is giving our shoes away to those who need them.

I particularly remember the first time the Lord prompted me to do this about thirty-five years ago. We were in a church service, and I knew of a young man who had just started a new job that required him to be on his feet all day. I asked how his new job was going, and he told me he loved his job, but his feet ached terribly. I had just bought a new pair of shoes the week before that were amazingly comfortable, and I loved those shoes. As we talked, I heard Holy Spirit say, "Tell him to try your shoes on." I took my shoes off and handed them over, saying what the Lord told me. As he slipped them on, he said, "Wow, Bobby, these are amazing!" I knew it was God and I replied, "That's awesome to hear, Eric, because they belong to you now." Oh, the joy of walking to my car that night in my socks!

This has happened a few other times as well, like when I took my shoes off in a parking lot to give to a homeless man Lisa and I just ministered to. The look on his face was that of shock as he took off his mismatched flip flops and I knelt to tie my shoes upon the man's feet.

Another time, Lisa was talking to a young new mom about her baby before church started. Lisa was wearing a pair of custom-stitched cowboy boots that she loved. The young girl noticed them and said to Lisa, "I love your boots; they are beautiful!" When the altar call was given at the end of service, this young mom went forward to give her life to Christ. When Lisa saw her at the front, she felt the prompting of the Holy Spirit to give this young mom her boots.

Lisa said to the Lord, "If that is you, Holy Spirit, tell me her name again." Immediately Lisa heard a whisper in her ear as God told her the young woman's name. Lisa didn't hesitate. She took off her boots and walked over and give them to the young mom, and yes, they were exactly her size!

These are simple acts of kindness that anyone could do. As you allow the fruit of kindness to develop in your spirit, you will become a cheerful giver, which is the outcome of the fruit of kindness.

Goodness: The Sixth Fruit of the Spirit

The Greek word for *goodness* is *agathosune*, which is the state of being good, virtuous, benevolent, generous and God-like in life and conduct. The manifestation of the fruit of the Spirit in our lives will at times seem very contrary to how we feel or want to act in certain situations. This is where we really learn to surrender our will to the Father's will.

There are a multitude of ways believers can produce the fruit of goodness in their lives. For example, by selflessly giving to others in need, sacrificing time to help others who have suffered a loss, and doing deeds motivated by the desire to bless.

During the early weeks of the Covid pandemic in 2020, I recall one time when Lisa accompanied me while I was helping a brother keep his business going by helping him restock some of his ATM machines with cash.

We were in a small neighborhood market to replenish the store's ATM with $10,000 in twenty-dollar bills, and because I had my back to the door as I was working, Lisa came in with me to watch my back. As I was resetting the machine, Lisa walked off and left me. I turned around to see what she was doing, and she had her arm around a little old lady who was standing near the front counter.

I heard Lisa ask her if she was afraid, and the woman said, "Yes, I'm very afraid, and I don't have enough money to feed my grandchildren." Then Lisa began to minister to the woman that God was a good God and she did not have to be afraid, while discreetly pulling out her credit card and handing it to the clerk behind the counter to pay for the older woman's groceries.

As Lisa prayed with the lady to receive the Lord Jesus into her heart, the clerk stood there dumbfounded as he watched the whole thing take place. He was of Arab descent, and I could tell he was questioning within himself why Lisa would pay for a complete stranger's groceries and comfort her when everybody except the two of us seemed to be paralyzed with fear.

When we act on God's behalf toward others, God is pleased; and what you do for others, God will do for you! The agape love of God compels the other fruit of the Spirit to manifest in every willing believer, and sometimes operating in the goodness of God requires laying down how you feel so that God's goodness displayed can bring about repentance.

> Or do you despise the riches of His goodness, forbearance, and longsuffering, not knowing that **the goodness of God leads you to repentance**? (Romans 2:4)

The fruit of God's goodness will cause your own life to be blessed.

Faithfulness/Faith: The Seventh Fruit of the Spirit

The next fruit of the Spirit is faithfulness or faith. The Greek word here, *pistis*, conveys the conviction or confidence that can have total trust and reliance in God and all He says.[3]

Faith is developed and grows as we hear the Word of God and get it down deep in our spirit. We hear, and we hear, and we hear—and then we do what we've heard. When we hear testimonies of miracles and healings, it causes our faith to grow as we develop an assurance that God is who He says He is and does what He says He can and will do.

> So faith comes by hearing [what is told], and what is heard comes by the preaching [of the message that came from the lips] of Christ (the Messiah Himself) (Romans 10:17 AMPC).

---

3. *Thayer and Smith's Greek Lexicon*, s.v. "Pistis," Bible Study Tools, accessed February 19, 2025, https://www.biblestudytools.com/lexicons/greek/kjv/pistis.html.

Faith in a believer is what moves God. And this is not manipulating God; our faith pleases God and He loves to respond to faith.

> Some people brought to him a paralyzed man on a mat. **Seeing their faith**, Jesus said to the paralyzed man, "Be encouraged, my child! Your sins are forgiven" (Matthew 9:2 NLT).

> Jesus turned around, and when he saw her he said, "Daughter, be encouraged! **Your faith** has made you well." And the woman was healed at that moment (Matthew 9:22 NLT).

> You can pray for anything, and if **you have faith**, you will receive it (Matthew 21:22 NLT).

> And Jesus said, "All right, receive your sight! **Your faith** has healed you" (Luke 18:42 NLT).

Through faith we act with boldness on what Jesus said and taught, just like Peter and John did when they healed the crippled man as they were going in for prayer. That miracle caused such a commotion that Peter used the moment to preach and declare to everyone who was listening that faith in Jesus' name has the same anointing that Jesus had to heal the sick.

> **Through faith in the name of Jesus**, this man was healed—and you know how crippled he

was before. **Faith in Jesus' name has healed him** before your very eyes (Acts 3:16 NLT).

Paul also preached powerfully by faith in Jesus' name, and his preaching produced faith for mighty miracles. Paul's bold declaration of faith prompted the confident response in the man who was crippled, and he jumped to his feet and started walking!

> While they were at Lystra, Paul and Barnabas came upon a man with crippled feet. He had been that way from birth, so he had never walked. He was sitting and listening as Paul preached. Looking straight at him, Paul realized **he had faith to be healed**. So Paul called to him in a loud voice, "Stand up!" And the man jumped to his feet and started walking (Acts 14:8-10 NLT).

We can strengthen our faith, be encouraged by faith, grow our faith, and use our faith to protect and shield us from the attacks of the enemy. Satan is defeated and overthrown by our faith!

> Then Judas and Silas, both being prophets, spoke at length to the believers, encouraging and **strengthening their faith** (Acts 15:32 NLT).

> Because of Christ and **our faith in him**, we can now come boldly and confidently into God's presence (Ephesians 3:12 NLT).

Our lives are blessed by the fruit of the Spirit and our faith is proof that the divine nature of God has been imparted to us. In addition to the *fruit* of faith is the power *gift* of faith, which we will study on later.

Gentleness: The Eighth Fruit of the Spirit

The Greek word for gentleness is *praotes*, which means, "gentleness, mildness, meekness,"[4] and conveys the idea of being even-balanced in tempers and passions and patient when suffering a wrong without feeling a spirit of revenge.

Not many people use the word gentleness (or meekness) anymore because it can be misinterpreted as timidity or failing to stand up for oneself—especially in the world we live in today, in which far too many have a "me first" attitude and selfishness is rampant.

Let's take a look at the story of the leper who came to Jesus to be healed in Matthew chapter 8 (which is a great chapter about healing). Lepers were outcasts—isolated to control the spread of the sickness they had. Many of these people had become lepers by no fault of their own; they contracted a very contagious disease and were no doubt heartbroken and cursed with fear, loneliness, rejection, and shame.

---

4. *Thayer and Smith's Greek Lexicon*, s.v. "Praotes," Bible Study Tools, accessed February 19, 2025, https://www.biblestudytools.com/lexicons/greek/kjv/praotes.html.

What Jesus did when the leper came to Him for healing is a beautiful display of His gentleness and agape love. Take a look and picture this interaction:

> And behold, a leper came and worshiped Him, saying, "Lord, if You are willing, You can make me clean." **Then Jesus put out His hand and touched him**, saying, "I am willing; be cleansed." Immediately his leprosy was cleansed (Matthew 8:2-3).

Jesus touched him—He laid hands on him—and said, "Be cleansed." Like I mentioned, leprosy was highly contagious, so the simple act of Jesus reaching out and touching the man in any way was an unexpected act of the agape love of God and gentleness. Obviously, Jesus was not afraid to touch the man or concerned that He might catch the disease. Jesus laid His hands on the leper out of great compassion and gentleness, and the man was immediately healed.

Gentleness breaks down walls that may not otherwise come down. Here are two more examples of gentleness from my own life.

My father-in-law was a World War II Navy veteran; he married my mother-in-law after they both had lost their first spouses and were widowed. Though they married later in life, they enjoyed another twenty-seven years together before he passed away at ninety-four years of age.

Lisa and I had ministered to Dad many times over the years, particularly in healing. His first wife had died from cancer, and he could never quite understand how when we prayed over him, he had been healed multiple times, yet she passed away even after receiving much prayer. He was very supportive of our ministry and loved us dearly, but he kept God at a distance because of that experience.

Easter Sunday morning two years before he passed, Lisa and I were at church, and as the service ended and we were about to leave, both of us received an unction from Holy Spirit that today was her father's day of salvation. We wasted no time driving to their home about forty-five minutes away, and after we said our hellos and brought in some fixings for dinner, Lisa asked her ninety-two-year-old father to go out on the sun porch with her while I kept her mom occupied in the kitchen. Lisa expressed to Dad how he had truly been a father to her for nearly a quarter of a century and how much she loved him. Holy Spirit had already gotten to Dad's heart, and he replied, "I love you, too, honey; you've saved my life several times."

Lisa gently corrected him and said, "No, Dad; Bobby and I prayed for you by faith in Jesus' name, but God healed you." She went on say, "I have something I want to talk to you about today as we celebrate His resurrection today. I want to know that you will be with us in heaven."

This was the first time in all the years we approached this subject that he responded, "Well, I want to believe I will be there too." That was all she needed.

Lisa said, "Dad, you can know you will be there if you will pray with me now and ask Jesus to be your Lord and Savior." After years and years, the gentleness of the Spirit broke through, and Dad gave his life to Jesus.

Two years later as he was about to pass, while I had my hand on his chest he said to me, "Bobby, if heaven is everything you said it will be, I will send you a sign." I smiled as I held back tears and said, "Dad, it will be far better than that, and you won't be able to send a sign, but that will be okay because I know you will be there when I get home."

Gentleness is a fruit of the Spirit that operates in our lives as a gift to others, and it's a joy when you allow this fruit to come alive in you.

Self-Control: The Ninth Fruit of the Spirit

The Greek word for self-control, *enkrateia,* refers to moderation in the indulgence of appetites and passions. Self-control is needed more today than at any other time in my lifetime. Without the fruit of self-control, it's easy to give in to selfishness, greed, overindulgence, and many forms of sinful behavior.

> But know this, that in the last days perilous times will come: For men will be lovers of themselves, lovers of money, boasters, proud, blasphemers, disobedient to parents, unthankful, unholy, unloving, unforgiving, slanderers, **without self-control**, brutal, despisers of

good, traitors, headstrong, haughty, lovers of pleasure rather than lovers of God, having a form of godliness but denying its power. And from such people turn away! (2 Timothy 3:1-5)

Self-control begins in our born-again spirit and then manifests or shows up in our outward lives. Until we are born again, our thoughts and actions will be out of control because we are driven by our senses (flesh). First, we think about things, and then we act on them—this is how all sin works. This is exactly how temptation was crafted by Satan to entrap Eve. The enemy got her to think about what he was presenting, and then she fell.

Then the serpent said to the woman, "You will not surely die. For God knows that in the day you eat of it your eyes will be opened, and you will be like God, knowing good and evil." So when the woman saw that the tree *was* good for food, that it *was* pleasant to the eyes, and a tree desirable to make *one* wise, she took of its fruit and ate. She also gave to her husband with her, and he ate (Genesis 3:4-6).

The Lord helped me greatly with this, and I still have to use the revelation of what He taught me when it comes to my own eating. I love to eat; I am a good ole' southern boy, and food is a part of everything we do. When I moved back home from being in Upstate New York for nearly thirty-eight years, I immediately gained weight—not just a little bit, but a good amount! Lisa actually said to me at one point, "Bobby, are you happy yet?"

I went right back to drinking sweet tea and eating fried everything, and because I was commuting seventy-five minutes to work and back, I had stopped working out like I had been doing before we moved. Lisa tried to help me when we went out to eat and would gently say things like, "You don't need the potatoes, or hush puppies, or dinner rolls," to which I would say, "Yeah, okay," but inside I was mad!

In a time of prayer, I asked Holy Spirit to help me get back on track and help me shed the weight and the bad attitude. The revelation He gave me empowered me because before He spoke to me, I was acting like a mad victim. He said, "When you are making food choices, stop saying, 'I can't eat that.' Say instead, 'I won't eat that.'"

This changed my entire perspective! Instead of feeling like I didn't have a say or choice, it empowered me to make a choice *and the right choice at that.* I no longer had anger and resentment from passing up the home fries or biscuits, and I felt empowered and happy with my choices and self-control.

When I began studying the fruits of the Spirit, I realized that the revelation He gave me was the fruit of self-control at work in my life.

> **It's not good to eat too much** honey, and it's not good to seek honors for yourself. A person

without self-control is like a city with bro-ken-down walls (Proverbs 25:27-28 NLT).

Better to be patient than powerful; better to have **self-control** than to conquer a city (Proverbs 16:32 NLT).

* * *

After looking deeper into the nine fruits of the Spirit, I hope you can start to recognize them at work in your life as you act according to His likeness. Like we talked about earlier, God breathed His breath into Adam in the garden and imparted His own divine nature into human-ity, and after we are born again, Holy Spirit indwells our spirit, and the fruit of Spirit is the supernatural outcome of that impartation.

Faith Declaration:

I choose to become a branch on the vine that manifests the fruit of the Spirit, the divine nature of God in my life: love, joy, peace, patience, kindness, goodness, faithfulness, gentleness, and self-control. To God be all the glory!

Chapter 4: Desire the Best Gifts

Now you are the body of Christ, and members individually. And God has appointed these in the church: first apostles, second prophets, third teachers, after that miracles, then gifts of healings, helps, administrations, varieties of tongues. Are all apostles? Are all prophets? Are all teachers? Are all workers of miracles? Do all have gifts of healings? Do all speak with tongues? Do all interpret? But earnestly desire the best gifts. And yet I show you a more excellent way (1 Corinthians 12:27-31).

I have so longed to get to this very point in this book because Lisa and I have ministered to the broken almost daily throughout our ministry, and the way the gifts of Holy Spirit work through our lives for the benefit of others gives us the greatest confidence that people's lives are about to forever change.

No one could ever convince me that the power of the Holy Spirit is not in full operation today because I have seen too many people healed of cancer, autoimmune diseases, and every other sort of sickness and disease. I've watched firsthand as people were set free and delivered from demonic strongholds, drugs, alcohol, and other addictions; not to mention marriages restored and total transformations through the power of the Holy Spirit to the glory of God. When we declare the name of the Lord Jesus, Holy Spirit confirms the authority of Jesus and miracles happen.

The Apostle Paul wrote much about the differences of ministries, activities, and the diversities of gifts given to the church by Holy Spirit. In his letters to the early church believers, Paul outlined different types of gifts, including the power gifts of the Spirit, gifts of service, administration, giving, teaching, being a leader, and so on. Paul described all these activities, "gifts differing according to the grace that is given to us." These are not natural abilities, although they may seem to flow naturally, but they are supernatural, spiritual giftings that function through a believer as well as those who are called into ministry to the benefit of the whole church.

> The human body has many parts, but the many
> parts make up one whole body. So it is with
> the body of Christ (1 Corinthians 14:12 NLT).

Paul used the metaphor of the human body to explain the diversity of Christ's body and how spiritual gifts that operate in the church work together much the same way as your foot, ankle, knee, and upper leg must naturally function together so you can walk.

> For as we have many members in one body, but all the members do not have the same function, so we, being many, are one body in Christ, and individually members of one another. Having then gifts differing according to the grace that is given to us, let us use them: if prophecy, let us prophesy in proportion to our faith; or ministry, let us use it in our ministering; he who teaches, in teaching; he who exhorts, in exhortation; he who gives, with liberality; he who leads, with diligence; he who shows mercy, with cheerfulness (Romans 12:4-8).

Paul also wrote to the Ephesians and revealed further instructions on how God set specific offices or those with distinct callings as gifts to the church. They had a specific responsibility and purpose in the church.

> Now these are the gifts Christ gave to the church: the apostles, the prophets, the evangelists, and the pastors and teachers. Their responsibility is to equip God's people to do his work and build up the church, the body of Christ. This will continue until we all come to such unity in our faith and knowledge of God's Son that we will be mature in the Lord, measuring up to the full and complete standard of Christ (Ephesians 4:11-13 NLT).

This passage describes what is commonly referred to as the "five-fold ministry gifts," which are given by the Lord to the church to equip God's people to do His work and build up the church, the body of Christ. The unique calling on the lives of those who serve in these offices is to help believers be ready for the work of the ministry, and those five-fold offices are to be carried out by believers who are full of the Spirit and wisdom. This is what the apostles meant by declaring in Acts 6:4 that they would continue to spend their time in prayer and teaching the word.

These five ministry gifts operate in the church today just as they did when Paul first wrote about them to the Ephesians because we still need to evangelize a lost world, preach about the forgiveness of sin, establish new works, and lead believers into the fullness of Christ.

The Holy Spirit (who is referred to as our Helper) is orchestrating all these diverse activities through those who are anointed and called to equip believers to do the work of the ministry. As in the days of the early church, sharing the gospel is taking place house to house, in the market squares, our places of work, our recreational ball fields, and all the other arenas of life. And I have never seen the fields of life so ripe for harvest as they are today.

Those you meet who work alongside you every day, serve you coffee, check you out at the grocery store, or sit next to you in the stands at your children's sporting events are all trying to outrun the burdens of life. They long to fill the emptiness that nags at their soul. Some try to outrun it for a while and fill that void with the world's goods, but that is fleeting and will eventually fade away. Most have no idea that the emptiness they so desperately want to fill can only be found in Christ.

This is where the work of the ministry actually takes place, when the people you talk to every day share their struggles, their worries and fears, and especially their hopes and dreams. This is why we *must* be equipped to do the work of the ministry. We have to be quick to listen and confident that God can and will intervene and show Himself faithful, but how can we do that if we are afraid to speak up or we are just as empty inside?

This is why we must be filled with power to be witnesses, just as Jesus said—baptized with the Holy Spirit and fire!

Just before he was taken up to heaven, Jesus Himself declared this is exactly how it would occur. Remember His disciples all received salvation and were born again on the night of His resurrection.

> And being assembled together with them, He commanded them not to depart from Jerusalem, but to wait for the Promise of the Father, "which," He said, "you have heard from Me; for John truly baptized with water, **but you shall be baptized with the Holy Spirit not many days from now**" (Acts 1:4-5).

That promise was fulfilled just a few days later on the day of Pentecost; Holy Spirit came in and filled each believer who was present!

> When the Day of Pentecost had fully come, they were all with one accord in one place. And suddenly there came a sound from heaven, as of a rushing mighty wind, and it filled the whole house where they were sitting. Then there appeared to them divided tongues, as of fire, and *one* sat upon each of them. **And they were all filled with the Holy Spirit and began to speak with other tongues, as the Spirit gave them utterance** (Acts 2:1-4).

This is an important key that must not be over-looked—praying in tongues is the spiritual language of God and is the gateway to the supernatural gifts of the Spirit flowing through believers today, just as it was in the early church. Like I mentioned earlier, there are those who teach and preach that the baptism in the Holy Spirit and His power is no longer needed or in operation today, but that is a completely false doctrine and a great error that has hindered many from receiving the fullness of Christ.

These same preachers and denominations agree that the fruit of the Spirit is in full operation and should be developed in the life of every believer today, but they teach the power gifts are no longer needed or in operation. Why would Holy Spirit indwell our born-again spirit and impart to us His nature without also infilling us with His power to be witnesses in the earth today just as it was in the beginning?

These folks further agree that the five-fold ministry gifts are still in operation today and fully expect that they should be recognized and honored in their churches, but the line in the sand for these preachers and denominations is Pentecost. They view Pentecost as if it were a one-and-done observance of a past experience rather than what Jesus said it is and what Paul taught it is still to be.

In the first chapter if this book we read over and over throughout the book of Acts how the baptism of Holy Spirit ignited the church with fresh power and the church spread out in every direction with signs and wonders following. In these last days, the presence of God we are to experience and operate in is to be even stronger and more glorious than what we read happened as the church came into existence. In fact, the prophet Haggai prophesied specifically about the glory of the last house being greater than at the beginning.

> The silver is Mine and the gold is Mine, says the Lord of hosts. The latter glory of this house [with its successor, to which Jesus came] shall be greater than the former, says the Lord of hosts; and in this place will I give peace *and* prosperity, says the Lord of hosts (Haggai 2:8-9 AMPC).

Paul encouraged believers to pray often in their prayer language and to count on Holy Spirit to help know what to pray when they have no words. We need this today more than ever!

> And the Holy Spirit helps us in our weakness. For example, **we don't know what God wants us to pray for. But the Holy Spirit prays for us with groanings that cannot be expressed in words**. And the Father who knows all hearts knows what the Spirit is saying, for the Spirit pleads for us believers in harmony with God's own will (Romans 8:26-27 NLT).

This is precisely why Paul, who wrote two thirds of the New Testament, prayed in tongues so often. He, too, needed supernatural revelation and guidance; in fact, he told the believers of the early church that he prayed in tongues more than anyone else.

> I thank God that I speak in tongues more than any of you (1 Corinthians 14:18 NLT).

The Apostle Paul received great spiritual insight directly from the Lord concerning the kingdom of God, our redemption by the blood, the revelation of who we are in Christ, how to cooperate with Holy Spirit in our everyday lives, and how to function in the anointing and gifts of the Spirit, but how did Paul come to know about all these things?

Paul gives the answer in the defense of his faith before King Agrippa. In the middle of his retelling of the encounter of what happened the day he met the Lord on the road to Damascus, Paul goes into greater detail than what we read in Acts chapter 9, and in verse 16 the Lord reveals that He will be showing Paul things that he needs to tell others.

> "Who are you, lord?" I asked. And the Lord replied, "I am Jesus, the one you are persecuting. Now get to your feet! For I have appeared to you to appoint you as my servant and witness. **Tell people that you have seen me, and tell them what I will show you in the future"** (Acts 26:15-16 NLT).

We see even more of what happened with Paul as he was writing to the Galatians.

> But I make known to you, brethren, that the gospel which was preached by me is not according to man. **For I neither received it from man, nor was I taught it, but it came through the revelation of Jesus Christ** (Galatians 1:11-12).

The Amplified Bible, Classic Edition says Paul received the gospel by a direct revelation given to him by Jesus Christ.

> For indeed I did not receive it from man, nor was I taught it, but [it came to me] through a **[direct] revelation [given] by Jesus Christ (the Messiah)** (Galatians 1:12 AMPC).

I'm certain that Holy Spirit did exactly this with Paul—and He still does with believers today. We can be confident of this because of what Jesus taught His disciples as He was preparing them for His departure. Jesus specifically told the apostles about the ministry of Holy Spirit, our Helper, whom He promised the Father would send to teach us, to show us things to come, and bring to our remembrance all things that Jesus said and taught.

> These things I have spoken to you while being present with you. But the Helper, the Holy Spirit, whom the Father will send in My name, **He will teach you all things**, and bring to your remembrance all things that I said to you (John 14:25-26).

> I still have many things to say to you, but you cannot bear them now. However, when He, the Spirit of truth, has come, He will guide you into all truth; for He will not speak on His own authority, but whatever He hears He will speak; and **He will tell you things to come** (John 16:12-13).

During the Last Supper with his disciples, Jesus said, "I still have many things to say to you, but you cannot bear them now." The reason they couldn't handle those things was because they weren't born again yet, and the things of the Spirit have to be received in the spirit, which is why Jesus continued by assuring that He was sending the Holy Spirit.

After his resurrection, Jesus spent forty days with the disciples sharing with them about the kingdom of God because now they could finally understand what he was telling them.

> To them also He showed Himself alive after His passion (His suffering in the garden and on the cross) by [a series of] many convincing demonstrations [unquestionable evidences and infallible proofs], **appearing to them during forty days and talking [to them] about the things of the kingdom of God**. And while being in their company *and* eating with them, He commanded them not to leave Jerusalem but to wait for what the Father had promised, Of which [He said] you have heard Me speak. For John baptized with water, but not many days from now you shall be baptized with (placed in, introduced into) the Holy Spirit (Acts 1:3-5 AMPC).

"Introduced into the Holy Spirit"—I love this wording, and that is exactly what happened to Paul after receiving the Holy Spirit. He went into the Arabian desert to receive direct revelation from the Lord and then returned and immediately began to teach the fullness of Christ, which he once persecuted and sought to destroy.

Under the inspiration of the Holy Spirit, Paul set in place much of the functionality of the church. He wrote letters to believers in the cities he had reached with the message of Jesus and set in order how the gifts of the Spirit were to operate. We are still in this dispensation known as the church age, so all that Paul set in order then should still be in operation today.

We still need the five-fold ministry gifts; we still need hospitality, administrations, giving, teaching, leadership, prophecy—and now more than ever we need the Holy Spirit and fire! Paul also wrote to the Corinthian believers about the nine power gifts that Holy Spirit distributes to each believer individually as He wills. Unlike the fruits of the Spirit, all of which every believer should be developing in their lives, no believer generally operates in all nine gifts of the Spirit.

> There are **diversities of gifts**, but the same Spirit. There are **differences of ministries**, but the same Lord. And there are **diversities of activities**, but it is the same God who works all in all. But the manifestation of the Spirit is given to each one for the profit of all: for to one is given the word of wisdom through the Spirit, to another the word of knowledge

through the same Spirit, to another faith by the same Spirit, to another gifts of healings by the same Spirit, to another the working of miracles, to another prophecy, to another discerning of spirits, to another different kinds of tongues, to another the interpretation of tongues. But one and the same Spirit works all these things, distributing to each one individually as He wills (1 Corinthians 12:4-11).

I emboldened the phrases **diversity of gifts, differences of ministries**, and **diversities of activities** because behind each of these phrases are three additional phrases. They are the terms **the same Spirit, the same Lord, and the same God.** The Father, the Son, and the Holy Spirit are all actively involved in the administration of the gifts of the Spirit. To dismiss the gifts as no longer in operation today requires dismissing the active involvement of God in any aspect of our lives.

It is not uncommon to find that some believers operate more frequently with great success in one or more of the nine gifts of the Spirit. It is not uncommon for some people to operate in several gifts in conjunction, such as prophecy with the word of knowledge, the word of wisdom, or the gifts of healings.

For instance, evangelists tend to operate with signs and wonders following the preaching of the gospel in their ministry because that is one of the ways the lost come to Christ. For this reason, the gifts of healings and the working of miracles very often operate together in the life of those called to be evangelists. We see this in Philip's ministry, for example, when he went down to Samaria—while he preached, people were healed and delivered from demons (see Acts 8:5-8).

The ministry of the prophet is composed of far more than just prophesying, although prophecy is the vehicle most often used to deliver a word of wisdom or a word of knowledge. Pastors and teachers have specific roles they are to accomplish in the local church, and for this reason, the gifts of prophecy, tongues and interpretation, and discerning of spirits may all at times manifest in their ministries along with the other gifts. Apostles who plant new churches or fellowships as the gospel spreads need to rely on the power gifts of Holy Spirit to fulfill their mission, so the gift of faith or other gifts necessary to develop and train leaders for these new works will be in operation in those ministers' lives and ministries.

Miracles, signs, and wonders should be the norm—not the exception—in a supernatural dynamic body of believers who are operating in the gifts of the Spirit. My purpose for reiterating that there are many gifts of the Spirit which have been given to believers is to prove that they should all still be operating in the body of Christ today as it was in the beginning.

In one of our opening Scripture passages, Paul encouraged the church to earnestly desire "the best gifts," as the King James Version says. Let's read this passage again so I can address another significant point that we will expound on in our next chapter as we discuss the gift of different kinds of tongues.

> Now you are the body of Christ, and members individually. And God has appointed these in the church: first apostles, second prophets, third teachers, after that miracles, then gifts of healings, helps, administrations, varieties of tongues. Are all apostles? Are all prophets? Are all teachers? Are all workers of miracles? Do all have gifts of healings? **Do all speak with tongues**? Do all interpret? But earnestly desire the best gifts. And yet I show you a more excellent way (1 Corinthians 12:27-31).

This is one of the scriptures that Cessationists (those who believe the gifts are no longer needed or in operation) love to use to distort the truth and bring confusion by misquoting the question, "Do all speak with tongues?"

It is amazing how they skip over, "Are all apostles, teachers, or evangelists," in the exact same passage! The obvious answer is no, we are not all apostles, teachers, or evangelists, but obviously these ministry gifts exist and function in the church today. This is why we need to study the Bible—read, reread, and cross reference what Paul's letters to the churches taught, viewing it as a consistent whole as the confirmation of Jesus' life ministry and teachings!

I started my career in telecom when I was a young man straight out of the military and before I went to Bible college. I was required to travel often for my job, and eventually one of the young men I traveled with decided to leave the company. The last time we traveled home together, he rededicated his life back to God, and as we were talking in his car, I gave him my Bible. As we talked, he opened my Bible to this particular passage above and said, "If tongues are still for today, then why does it ask right here, 'Do all have the ability to speak in tongues?' My old pastor said we don't do this anymore." He had walked in on me praying in tongues several times while I was working and said, "I can't deny its real; I've heard you doing it for months when you are praying, but I don't think it's for everybody."

I became born again just before I got out of the military, and even though I loved the Lord and had gotten baptized in the Spirit thirteen days after I was saved, I did not know enough of the Word to answer his question properly that night. In fact, I didn't know the difference until I went to Bible college. All I could say at the time was, "If He filled me, I don't know why you think God wouldn't fill you too."

I knew inside my own spirit that there was more to what Paul was saying to the Corinthians, I just didn't know what it was yet. I wasn't satisfied with my answer, and that night caused me to burn with a deeper desire to learn and be able to give a proper account of my salvation and learn everything I could about the Holy Spirit and His gifts.

Just two months after Lisa and I got married, we started attending Bible college, and the quest to know how to answer questions like my buddy asked in the car that night really began to take shape. That quest to learn has now spanned more than forty years and will continue throughout the rest of my life.

Faith Declaration

Holy Spirit, I desire for You fill me with the best gifts now. I refuse to limit how and when You work through me to reach the world I live in with the fullness of Christ. I will prophesy and I will see the gifts manifest in my life because You want it to be so today just as it was in the early Church. I will be filled again and again with Your Spirit!

Chapter 5: Holy Spirit Infills Part 1

But the manifestation of the Spirit is given to each one for the profit of all: for to one is given the **word of wisdom** through the Spirit, to another the **word of knowledge** through the same Spirit, to another **faith** by the same Spirit, to another **gifts of healings** by the same Spirit, to another the **working of miracles**, to another **prophecy**, to another **discerning of spirits**, to another different kinds of **tongues**, to another the **interpretation of tongues**. But one and the same Spirit works all these things, distributing to each one individually as He wills (1 Corinthians 12:7-11).

As I said in our last chapter, Lisa and I headed off to Bible college less than eight weeks after we got married back in 1985. However, from the first few weeks after we met in church the year before, our "date nights" (actually anytime we were together) always seemed to center around sharing the good news of the gospel. Everywhere we went, whether it was city hall, downtown, county fairs, amusement parks, ballfields, or basketball courts, if crowds were gathered, Lisa and I were there too.

People will tell you an awful lot if you just listen before you speak; then Holy Spirit will show you what to say and it will be anointed to break through their struggles and bring the answer they need. It's amazing how many young people would seek us out after a Friday night high school football game and bring their friends to us to pray with them too!

During these times of street evangelism, Lisa and I both began to notice the gifts of the Spirit regularly manifesting in our lives. When your desire is to lift up the name of Jesus, Holy Spirit will always be there because His ministry to the church is to glorify the Lord Jesus!

One of the first times that Lisa received a word of knowledge happened while she was out for a training run. A car full of young boys began heckling her while she ran and even pulled into a parking lot and got out of their car. As they approached her, a boldness rose up in her and she received a word of knowledge right there in the parking lot. One of the most vocal boys was walking toward Lisa when she was apprehended by the Holy Spirit and pointed right at him and called him by name. He was visibly shaken by that and immediately asked her with a quivering voice, "How...how do you know my name?"

Lisa said, "I saw your name written right above your head as soon as you got out of the car." Then she grabbed his hand and said, "Give your life to Christ right now!" He did not jerk his hand away from her; in fact, he was overwhelmed and appeared like he truly wanted to pray. His friends were so shocked and scared that they took off running back to their car, calling for the boy, who ran back to the car and got in quickly before they sped away.

I will share one more quick story of how Holy Spirit began working in our lives right from our earliest days of ministry. One Saturday morning we went to Sylvan Beach, a small amusement park on Oneida Lake in Upstate New York. Lisa and I had been sharing the gospel and witnessed quite a few folks give their hearts to the Lord. While we were at the amusement park, I had joined a three-on-three basketball game, which I often enjoyed doing, and after we finished our game we talked with the guys for a short bit and then prayed with them all.

It was about midday by this time, and Lisa and I decided to take a walk down the midway of the park. It was hot out, so Lisa sat down on some steps with our daughter Marla to rest while we discussed what we wanted to eat. My young son Aaron sat on my shoulders as we talked. What we didn't realize was that the steps Lisa and our daughter Marla sat down on were part of a fortune teller's booth, complete with a big crystal ball.

Within seconds, the fortune teller yanked open the black curtains from behind her stage and shouted at us, "I know who you are and what spirit you're of, now get off my steps!"

We turned around to see who was yelling at us and without hesitation, Lisa stood up, pointed her finger at the woman, and said, "You foul, unclean spirit, shut up and come out of her!" The boldness of Lisa's words scared the fortune teller so much that she gasped, screamed in fear as she pulled the curtain shut, and quickly scurried away.

It didn't really take the discerning of spirits to know what spirit she was of, but the courage to confront and rebuke her came from being baptized with the Holy Spirit and fire! As we grabbed our belongings and continued walking down the midway, our daughter Marla looked up at us and said, "The devil is scared of Jesus!" The spiritual world we live in, whether acknowledged or not, is far more genuine than the world we can see—and spiritual beings, both angelic and demonic, who operate in that realm are very aware of who we are.

It was no surprise to us that the women operating under the influence of an unclean spirit knew who we were because of the Holy Spirit dwelling in us. This happened in Jesus' ministry multiple times as well.

> Now there was a man in their synagogue with **an unclean spirit. And he cried out, saying**, "Let *us* alone! What have we to do with You, Jesus of Nazareth? Did You come to destroy us? **I know who You are—the Holy One of God!**" But Jesus rebuked him, saying, "Be quiet, and come out of him!" (Mark 1:23-25)

And he cried out with a loud voice and said, **"What have I to do with You, Jesus, Son of the Most High God?** I implore You by God that You do not torment me." For He said to him, "Come out of the man, unclean spirit!" (Mark 5:7-8)

Once we are born again by faith and baptized with the Holy Spirit and fire, we can begin to walk in the fullness of that blessing, just as it was when Adam walked with God before the fall, and just as Abraham did by faith after the blood covenant was established. Jesus became the curse of sin on the cross for us so we could receive the promise of the Spirit by faith just like Abraham had to when God pronounced the same blessing over Abraham that He had declared over Adam.

Christ has redeemed us from the curse of the law, having become a curse for us (for it is written, "Cursed *is* everyone who hangs on a tree"), **that the blessing of Abraham might come upon the Gentiles in Christ Jesus, that we might receive the promise of the Spirit through faith** (Galatians 3:13-14).

The Gifts of the Spirit

Much of what we are about to discuss concerning the power gifts of the Spirit, Lisa and I learned in Bible college from the required reading materials of Dr. Kenneth E. Hagin, a mighty man of God. Lisa and I are very thankful for all we learned from him. I will always be grateful for his ministry and forever cherish the memory of him laying hands on Lisa and I at an All Faiths Crusade in Detroit, Michigan many years ago in the fall of 1988.

> There are diversities of gifts, but the same Spirit. There are differences of ministries, but the same Lord. And there are diversities of activities, but it is the same God who works all in all. But the manifestation of the Spirit is given to each one for the profit of all: for to one is given the **word of wisdom** through the Spirit, to another the **word of knowledge** through the same Spirit, to another **faith** by the same Spirit, to another **gifts of healings** by the same Spirit, to another the **working of miracles**, to another **prophecy**, to another **discerning of spirits**, to another different kinds of **tongues**, to another the **interpretation of tongues**. But one and the same Spirit works all these things, distributing to each one individually as He wills (1 Corinthians 12:4-11).

The nine gifts of the Spirit are listed together by purpose and function, which will make them easier to study and also easier to remember. These gifts function in three sets of three as follows:

1. Gifts of revelation / gifts that **reveal** something

- Word of wisdom
- Word of knowledge

- Discerning of spirits

2. Gifts of power / gifts that **do** something

- Gift of faith
- Working of miracles
- Gifts of healings

3. Gifts of utterance / gifts that **say** something

- Prophecy
- Diverse or different kinds of tongues
- Interpretation of tongues

As we begin our study, it is vital to understand that these nine gifts are for equipping believers. These gifts are not just for those who serve in the five-fold ministry; otherwise, Paul would not have encouraged all believers to desire the best gifts. Brother Hagin used to say it this way, "What is the best gift? It's whatever gift you need at the time."

The Revelation Gifts

Word of Wisdom

Of the nine gifts the Spirit, the word of wisdom is the most important of all the gifts because it is a supernatural revelation of the mind and purpose of God communicated by Holy Spirit to man. It is predictive in that it reveals future events; it is not the whole counsel of God but only a part of God's wisdom. It is a "word" much like a word is part of a sentence, which is part of a paragraph, which is part of a book, which is part of a library.

A word of wisdom is a specifically revealed portion of God's plans, purposes, and His will that is yet to come. It is not the same as wisdom that is learned from much study. It is not experiential wisdom from years of doing or practicing. It is not naturally gained wisdom of any kind. Though God does guide believers through the wisdom gained by all these methods, the gift of the word of wisdom is a supernatural revelation of a part of God's wisdom that He specifically wants revealed and known at that particular moment in time.

A word of wisdom is divinely imparted directly to a believer and can come through any of several different means. Throughout the Bible, we see the word of wisdom delivered by angels, in visions, in dreams, by an audible voice, and through prophets and believers.

By angels:

- Gideon received a word of wisdom when the Angel of the Lord called him a mighty man of valor and then told him God's plan to use him to deliver Israel from the Midianites (Judges 6:11-16).

- Mary received a word of wisdom when the angel Gabriel told her she would bring forth the Son of God and what to name the child (Luke 1:26-33).

- Phillip after he ministered to the Samaritans received a word of wisdom when an angel of the

Lord told Phillip to go down to the desert for God had a purpose for Phillip to minister to an Ethiopian eunuch (Acts 8:26-29).

Through visions:

- Daniel who had been fasting and praying received a word of wisdom through a vision concerning events that were certain to happen in the last days. In this vision Daniel was visited by the angel Gabriel who was sent by God to help Daniel understand the vision (Daniel 10:1-21). Most of Daniel's revelations came through visions.

- Ananias received a word of wisdom directly from the Lord in a vision and was instructed to go lay hands on Saul, who was God's chosen vessel, and as he laid his hands on Paul he received his sight and was filled with the Holy Spirit (Acts 10:9-18).

In dreams:

- Joseph the son of Jacob received multiple words of wisdom that came through dreams and also the ability to interpret others' dreams by the word of wisdom. Genesis 37 through Genesis 42 cover multiple dreams and how the Lord spoke a word of wisdom through each of them to Joseph about God's plans, purposes, and will for Joseph.

- Joseph the husband of Mary received a word of wisdom when an angel of the Lord appeared to him in a dream and told him of God's plan to take Mary and Jesus and flee to Egypt because King Herod sought to kill the young child (Matthew 2:13-15). This also fulfilled the word of the Lord spoken by the prophet Hosea in Hosea 11:1.

By an audible voice:

- Samuel as a young boy in the temple heard the audible voice of the Lord and received a word of wisdom concerning the coming judgment on the prophet Eli and his wicked sons (1 Samuel 3:10-18).

- Saul on the road to Damascus heard the audible voice of the Lord when Jesus asked him, "Saul, Saul why are you persecuting Me?" Afterward Jesus said, "Arise, go into the city and you will be told what you must do" (Acts 9:3-6).

- John the Apostle on the isle of Patmos received the greatest word of wisdom concerning the plans, purposes, and will of the Lord. Jesus spoke to John and said: "I am the alpha and the Omega, the beginning and the end, who is and who was and who is to come, the almighty." And then He revealed the condition of the seven churches in Asia. John could not have otherwise known what was going on except by the word of the Lord (Revelation chapters 1-3).

The word of wisdom is a supernatural revelation of what God wants known, and Holy Spirit uses any means He deems fit to make sure you receive. Lisa and I have received several notable words of wisdom over the years. One such word came through a church member on Sunday morning shortly after we graduated from Bible college.

A sister in the Lord named Mary had approached us while we were standing in the back of the church and said, "I have a word for you. Can I share it with you?" We knew her well and trusted her, so we both answered, "Yes, of course." Then Mary began to explain how she had a dream the night before and in the dream she saw our baby daughter. She said, "I saw your daughter. She was beautiful and perfect, in every way strong and healthy."

At the time, we had two children—our son, Aaron, and our daughter, Marla—and we were not planning to have any more children. We had a boy and a girl and were content with our little family. We said, "Thank you, Mary, that's interesting, but we're not planning on having any more children." However, something about it grabbed hold of both Lisa and me as we talked about it later.

We had been taught in Bible college that when hearing a word of wisdom, unless we had a confirmation already in our heart, we should let that word sit on a proverbial shelf and wait to see if anything else came of it, or we should throw it away. Well, about two years later we did decide to have one more child, and after our son Timothy was born, we remembered the dream Mary shared with us and said, "Maybe she just had too much pizza the night before," and dismissed it with a chuckle.

About fourteen months later, Lisa became pregnant with our daughter Emily, and we once again recalled what Mary had said to us. Just before Emily's birth, the doctors discovered what they diagnosed as supraventricular tachycardia, which is a heart condition that causes rapid heartrates and can be fatal in infants. Now that word of wisdom that Mary spoke to us years before we needed it—and certainly before we understood its significance to us—came back in force and we declared the word of the Lord with confident boldness: "I saw your daughter. She is beautiful and perfect, in every way strong and healthy."

Today Emily is a young woman, and she is totally and completely whole. She is every bit what the Lord said: beautiful and perfect, in every way strong and healthy!

Another notable word of wisdom we received came as Lisa and I prepared to relocate to Florida several years ago from upstate New York. Although we wanted to move, we also had some concerns, and as we sought the Lord, He used both a word of knowledge and a word of wisdom to supernaturally confirm His plans, purpose, and will for why He was bringing us to Florida.

While in prayer one day, Lisa received divine direction for us to visit a certain city and church in Florida. We booked flights that same day and flew down in obedience. After looking up some information and the address for the church, we found that the church was in the third week of a revival and planned to attend as many services as we could while there, not knowing a single person in the church.

During the second night of the three services we attended, the prophet who was preaching walked over to us and stared at us intently and then went back to preaching. When he approached us a second time, he called us out and said, "I need you to come up here. I have a word for you." Then with extreme accuracy that only Lisa and I would have known, he began to reveal things of the past and present through a word of knowledge, which we will study next.

Now he had our full attention, and with a word of wisdom he revealed very specific details and things concerning our future, and I can tell you *everything he spoke has already come to pass* or we are in the middle of watching it unfold even now, including why God called us to Florida. As I am writing this this book, we recently placed a purchase offer on one hundred and forty six acres of land in North Florida, which will be the home of our ministry, the Open Skies Ranch, just as it was revealed by the word of wisdom, "I am bringing you to Florida to do ministry and everything you put your hand to, the Lord says He will be in it with you." That minister was Prophet Charlie Shamp, and the church was the River Clermont, where we started attending after we moved to Florida.

Oh, how many lives could be changed if the church would just allow Holy Spirit to be who Jesus said He would be before He ascended back to heaven! He is the Spirit of truth and He does, in fact, tell us things to come.

> However, when He, the Spirit of truth, has come, He will guide you into all truth; for He will not speak on His own *authority,* but whatever He hears He will speak; and He will tell you things to come (John 16:13).

Word of Knowledge

The word of knowledge is very similar to a word of wisdom in that it is also a supernatural revelation that reveals a part of God's knowledge that He specifically wants revealed and known at that time. It is a companion gift and operates very similar to the word of wisdom, except the word of knowledge reveals facts about past or present circumstances or things. It is not all knowledge or all knowing about your past or present circumstances but only as a single frame from an entire motion picture; it is only a fragment of God's unlimited knowledge that He reveals for a specific purpose.

It is not knowledge we learn by study, experience, or practice; it is a supernatural revealing of an event or circumstance that could not otherwise be known. This is exactly what happened when Lisa and I went to the River Clermont Church, having never even heard of the church until we flew down to Florida as directed by Holy Spirit.

The things that were spoken to us by Prophet Charlie Shamp, no one else but God could have been aware of or known. They were not random ideas, but two specific incidents that took place, including the exact words from the first incident a few years before that night. God used the word of knowledge coupled with a word of wisdom to supernaturally confirm His will for us to move to Florida and why.

As with all the gifts of the Spirit, it will certainly get your attention when specific knowledge of an event or person is revealed by Holy Spirit. This is what happened to Nathanael when Phillip went to get him so he could meet Jesus.

> Now Philip was from Bethsaida, the city of Andrew and Peter. Philip found Nathanael and said to him, "We have found Him of whom Moses in the law, and also the prophets, wrote—Jesus of Nazareth, the son of Joseph." And Nathanael said to him, "Can anything good come out of Nazareth? Philip said to him, "Come and see." Jesus saw Nathanael coming toward Him, and said of him, "Behold, an Israelite indeed, in whom is no deceit!" Nathanael said to Him, "How do You know me?" Jesus answered and said to him, "Before Philip called you, when you were under the fig tree, I saw you." Nathanael answered and said to Him, "Rabbi, You are the Son of God! You are the King of Israel!" Jesus answered and

said to him, "Because I said to you, 'I saw you under the fig tree,' do you believe? You will see greater things than these." And He said to him, "Most assuredly, I say to you, hereafter you shall see heaven open, and the angels of God ascending and descending upon the Son of Man" (John 1:44-51).

This is not only a great example of a word of knowledge, but also shows how it works together with the word of wisdom as companion gifts of the Spirit. First Jesus said to Nathanael, "Before Philip called you, when you were under the fig tree, I saw you." Jesus was not with Phillip, and He didn't talk to Phillip. The only way Jesus could have known Nathanael was sitting under a fig tree (a present fact) was by a word of knowledge.

Then Jesus said to him, "Most assuredly, I say to you, hereafter you shall see heaven open, and the angels of God ascending and descending upon the Son of Man." This truth was revealed by a word of wisdom; it was a future event that Jesus foretold would occur, and throughout Jesus' earthly ministry it happened just as He said it would.

Some might say, "Well, that was Jesus; He knows all things." But this is not true. The scriptures state that Jesus emptied Himself when He came to the earth, and that He grew in wisdom and stature. If Jesus had not set aside His omniscience, He would have had no need to grow in wisdom. Jesus depended on the Holy Spirit exactly the way we have to. He did this so He could show us how to function by the anointing of the Holy Spirit and flow in His leading.

Jesus never ceased to be God but willingly took on the flesh of mankind and functioned on earth as a man in every way like us. Fully God and yet fully man, Jesus, born of the Holy Spirit, functioned in His earthly ministry by the anointing of the Holy Spirit and operated in the gifts of the Spirit, just as we are expected to do. In His image and according to His likeness, we are to look and act like Jesus!

The gifts of the Spirit are not natural gifts that work through our natural minds by learned knowledge or experiential wisdom. As I stated earlier, the gifts are supernatural manifestations given by the Holy Spirit. There is no such thing as a gift of knowledge or a gift of wisdom; there is only a word of knowledge or the word of wisdom given directly by Holy Spirit to reveal a specific matter or purpose. Furthermore, there's no time limit on the word revealed, as was the case with the word of wisdom our friend Mary released to us nearly four years before we needed to know how to stand in confident assurance for our daughter Emily.

Abram received the promise of Issac as word of wisdom more than twenty years before, and because Abram believed God, his name was changed to Abraham (the father of nations) even before the promise manifested with the birth of Issac still many years off.

Whatever God gives by revelation is for a divine purpose, whether it concerns past or present events as a word of knowledge or future events concerning the will of God as a word of wisdom. Again, these gifts are companions and are very similar except for what they reveal and the timing of them—past, present, or future.

By these gifts and the others we have yet to study we participate in the realm of the Spirit according to God's *kairos* time and timing. Kairos is God's time, which is measured as set times, seasons, and appointed times, and is eternal. Kairos has no limitations to past, present, or future, which is how Holy Spirit is able to reveal to us past or present facts as well as the future plans and purposes of God directly to our born-again spirit.

Chronos is the natural time of God created for man, which is measured in minutes, hours, years, and so on. The chronological times of man are often interrupted by the "kairological" times of God when heaven and earth come together for the divine purposes of God in the spirit realm.

Discerning of Spirits

The discerning of spirits is the last of the revelation gifts and the seventh gift of the Spirit listed in 1 Corinthains 12:4-11. It is probably the most mischaracterized gift because it is not only about discerning evil spirits. Discerning of spirits gives supernatural insight into both the heavenly and demonic realms of the spirit world. As with all the gifts of the Spirit, this gift is supernatural and depends on no human understanding or natural intuition to function. Holy Spirit determines when it is necessary to allow us to see into the spirit realm.

To *discern* means to receive by either seeing or hearing, and so it is with discerning of spirits; you are enabled to see or hear in the realm of spirits. There are three classes of spirits that the discerning of spirits deals with: divine, satanic, and human. Here is what this gift allows the believer to do:

- Enabled to see angels, cherubim and seraphim, archangels, the host of heavenly angels, the similitude of God or the risen Christ, or even the discerning of Holy Spirit.

- Enabled to see a demon, a familiar spirit, Satan, or his disgraced legions of fallen angels.

- Have the ability to see into someone's disposition, intentions, motives, and their good or evil tendencies. They may also see the presence of a demon power possessing or oppressing a person or causing a specific condition or sickness.

The discerning of spirits is narrow in scope as it is specific to seeing into the spirit realm only, whereas the other two revelation gifts, the word of wisdom and the word of knowledge, apply to a much broader scope that includes people, places, and things. It is important to make this distinction because when you are operating in the gift of discerning of spirits you will see into the spirit realm. However, when the word of knowledge is in operation, you may know that a spirit is presently operating in a person, but would not see it.

Examples of seeing into the realm of the spirit include:

- John being able to see Jesus appearing before him on the isle of Patmos (Revelation 1:19-18).

- Stephen seeing the Lord Jesus sitting at the right hand of God just before he was martyred (Acts 7:55-57).

- Elisha's young servant who was able to see the angelic host sent to protect them when his eyes opened to see that the hillside was filled with horses and chariots of fire (2 Kings 6:15-17).

An example of knowing that a spirit is present by the word of knowledge is when Paul and Silas were in Philippi and certain slave girl was possessed with a spirit of divination. As she followed them, she was telling everyone, "These men are the servants of the Most High God, who proclaim to us the way of salvation." The slave girl was not an evangelist—far from it. She was doing this to confuse the people as to what spirit she was of, like the fortune teller woman at the amusement park in Sylvan Beach. The Bible says she did this for many days and Paul, after becoming greatly annoyed, turned and said to the spirit, "I command you in the name of Jesus Christ to come out of her." And the spirit came out that very hour (Acts 16:16-18).

Over the years of hearing Brother Hagin preach on the radio, on television, and in person, he shared many examples of the gift of the discerning of spirits operating in his ministry. After hearing so many examples, it was easy to know when we are experiencing the discerning of spirits firsthand.

One day Lisa and I brought a friend of ours and his wife with us to see the property that will soon become the Open Skies Ranch. This man is a prophet, and as we rode through the property he began to weep. When we drove past a particular spot, he asked me to turn around and slowly go back toward that location.

I watched his lip begin to quiver as he was trying to speak. He eventually got the words out and said, "I see a warring angel posted right there," pointing to a specific clump of trees. "He has a sword in his hand and has been posted here to secure this land for generations to come for the purpose of your ranch. He has been here many years waiting for this season."

That was the discerning of spirits in operation coupled with a word of wisdom as he saw into the realm of the spirit. The purpose of that manifestation was to strengthen our faith and to glorify God for what was about to come. This is why it is more critical than ever before to understand the power that has been given to the church through Holy Spirit and His gifts.

The purpose of His gifts is to equip believers with the power to bind the strong man and plunder his house, defeat the wicked one, and to set mankind free from the bondages of poverty, sin, sickness, and death just as Jesus did when

He walked the earth. It is foolish to believe that sin in all its manifestations is still in full operation on the earth today but all Holy Spirit's manifestations of power have ceased.

God does not and will not ever change. His power and authority are still above all powers and principalities. There is only one Holy Spirit, and He is still doing today what He did in the early church through those who believe.

> And He said to them, "Go into all the world and preach the gospel to every creature. He who believes and is baptized will be saved; but he who does not believe will be condemned. And these signs will follow **those who believe**: In My name they will cast out demons; they will speak with new tongues; they will take up serpents; and if they drink anything deadly, it will by no means hurt them; they will lay hands on the sick, and they will recover" (Mark 16:15-18).

Read again what Jesus said. **"These signs will follow those who believe. In My name they will...."** We are the "they" and we are "those who believe." There is no expiration date on believing any more than there is an expiration date on salvation. Jesus commissioned the disciples to teach and preach what belonged to all those who believe! If you are saved, then you have the authority to be casting out devils, speaking in new tongues, and healing the sick!

Faith Declaration

I am a believer, and these signs will follow me. I will cast out devils, speak in tongues, and lay hands on the sick and see them recover. I desire the best gifts of the Holy Spirit to work in me and through me.

Chapter 6: Holy Spirit Infills Part 2

The Spirit of God, who raised Jesus from the dead, lives in you. And just as God raised Christ Jesus from the dead, he will give life to your mortal bodies by this same Spirit living within you (Romans 8:11 NLT).

Wen Paul was writing to the church in Rome, he charged them to understand that the same Spirit that raised Christ from the dead now lived in them, just as Jesus promised it would be when He commanded them to stay in Jerusalem until they received. There is not a "God Holy Spirit" and then a "junior Holy Spirit" for man; no! The same Holy Spirit who anointed Jesus with power lives inside every believer.

And you know that God anointed Jesus of Nazareth with the Holy Spirit and with power. Then Jesus went around doing good and healing all who were oppressed by the devil, for God was with him (Acts 10:38 NLT).

We are to do the same thing with the same power through the same Holy Spirit. We have never been told to expect less or to accept less; in fact, read what Jesus told His disciples and all believers:

> Most assuredly, I say to you, he who believes in Me, the works that I do he will do also; and greater *works* than these he will do, because I go to My Father. And whatever you ask in My name, that I will do, that the Father may be glorified in the Son. If you ask anything in My name, I will do *it*. "If you love Me, keep My commandments. And I will pray the Father, and He will give you another Helper, **that He may abide with you forever**— the Spirit of truth, whom the world cannot receive, because it neither sees Him nor knows Him; but you know Him, for He dwells with you and will be in you (John 14:12-17).

How long will Holy Spirit abide with us? Forever! Never, ever, ever let anyone talk you out of this most precious promise straight from the mouth of Jesus. Holy Spirit will be with us forever and is still doing today all He did yesterday! Let us now continue our study on the power gifts of the Spirit.

The Power Gifts

Gift of Faith

The gift of faith is the first of the three power gifts and is the greatest of the three. The gift of faith enables a believer to sustain an unwavering trust in God's supernatural protection and provision and for receiving miracles. The gift of faith is passive in that it is the act of *receiving* miracles, whereas the working of miracles is active in the act of *creating* miracles.

The gift of faith is not a supercharged version of a believer's faith. It is a supernatural manifestation of God's faith operating in and through the life of a believer. The gift of faith is too often lumped in by some who make the assumption that all faith is the same just like all prayer is the same, but that is a big misconception in both cases.

There is saving faith, as in Ephesian 2:8-10, which is a gift of God's grace to bring the lost to salvation. There is general faith, which is the believer's faith in God, His word, and in all His promises. We are also expected to grow our faith (Romans 10:17), and we are expected to use our faith to please God and to be assured that He is the rewarder of those who live by faith (Hebrews 11:6).

We please God when we walk by faith; faith moves God. This is not a way to manipulate God—quite the opposite. Our faith touches God; it's a matter of the heart. Faith is the essential element of our existence; by faith we receive the Holy Spirit and by faith we receive the gifts of the same Holy Spirit. However, the *gift of faith* is a completely different manifestation. It's God's supernatural faith working through a believer.

Smith Wigglesworth certainly was a mighty man of faith who is credited with nearly twenty cases of raising the dead back to life in his ministry. He said if you take a step of ordinary faith, when you come to the end of that faith, very often the supernatural gift of special faith will take over. He went on to explain that one reason more folks don't see the manifestation of special faith operating in their lives is because they don't first use the faith they already have.

The gift of faith, or as Wigglesworth called it, "special faith," enables a believer to sustain an unwavering trust in God for personal protection, provision, and for receiving miracles. There are many examples of the gift of faith in operation in both the Old and New Testaments.

- Elijah received supernatural provision from God when he was fed daily by ravens at Kerith Brook. This was a supernatural trust in God to provide based on what God had spoken to him (1 Kings 17:1-6).

- The widow of Zarephath received supernatural provision for her jar of flour and her jug of oil because she kept the word of the Lord spoken by Elijah. Her provision never ran out during the drought until the Lord sent rain again on the land (1 Kings 17:13-16).

- We see the gift of faith operating for receiving miracles through the apostles who were sent to lay hands on the new believers in Samaria to receive the Holy Ghost with the evidence of speaking in tongues (Acts 8:14-17).

- Peter passively received a supernatural miracle through the gift of faith on the night before he was to be executed when God sent an angel to free Peter from his chains and escort him past the prison guards because the church prayed earnestly for his release (Acts 12:6-10).

The gift of faith can sustain and remain in operation as long as necessary. Elijah was sustained by ravens for about forty days. The widow of Zarephath received provision for nearly three years. Daniel's life was sustained for a night in the lion's den. Shadrach, Meshach, and Abed-Nego were supernaturally protected from the blazing furnace for maybe an hour. The new believers in Samaria saw instant answers to prayer. And Peter's supernatural protection lasted a few quick minutes until he was safely beyond the prison gates.

The gift of faith can hold back rain, like with Elijah, until God allows it to rain again. It can cause a supernatural hundredfold miracle harvest, like Isaac reaped during a period of severe famine. The gift of faith will also provide, protect, and cause miracles at the appointed time for you or those you are ministering to, through the power of the Holy Spirit!

My friend Brad Flook is an evangelist who ministers very often in Central America. He shared a testimony of how a bus he was riding on years ago was commandeered off the road by gunmen, who entered the bus and ordered all the men to get off. He shared how Holy Spirit told him to be still and not to get off the bus. The gunmen entered the bus a second time and ordered all the women off the bus, and again, as ordered by the Lord, Brad did not move.

A third time, the gunmen entered the empty bus and looked all around. Brad continued to sit in his seat while the gunmen walked all around him—*and never saw him sitting motionless in his seat the entire time!* This was a manifestation of the supernatural gift of faith for divine protection in operation. Brad did exactly as the Lord instructed and passively received a miracle. Brad is still preaching and seeing mighty signs and wonders in his ministry because he received then, and still receives today, many miracles by the gift of special faith.

Howard Carter so eloquently stated that the gift of faith calls into operation the powers of the world to come and unites angels with men for the accomplishment of God's divine purposes here in the earth.

Working of Miracles

The gift of the working of miracles is the second of the three power gifts and is often confused with the gifts of healings. This is a common misconception, so let me quickly explain the difference as it was taught to me. The gifts of healings heal what has been damaged, diseased, or broken, whereas the working of miracles creates, controls, or alters the laws of nature.

In the case of a deaf ear, for example, if the hearing loss was due to an injury or accident, the gifts of healings would be used to heal and restore what was lost. If the deaf ear is because an ear drum or auditory nerve never existed, then the working of miracles would be needed to create what never existed. As we continue our study on these gifts, we will certainly come to understand the difference between the two.

The working of miracles can best be described as a manifestation whereby the laws of nature are altered, suspended, controlled, or which creates what did not exist (except in the sphere of sickness and disease. As I stated, we will discuss this later as we study the gift of healings.

The manifestations of the working of miracles were more in evidence throughout the Old Testament because that was how God proved His presence and power. Those miracles established His divine authority before the peoples of the earth. Moses operated predominantly in this gift. The miracles established his credentials before

Pharoah—proof that Moses had been sent by God with power and authority.

We discussed earlier how, after a three-year drought caused by the spoken word of Elijah, God instructed Elijah to gather the people of Israel on Mount Carmel. After a dreadful display of failure of the part of the false prophets of Baal, Elijah called down fire from heaven that burned up the altar, the sacrifice, the wood, the stones, and even the water around the altar. God used this manifestation of the working of miracles to cause the people of Israel to repent and turn away from their sinful idol worship of Baal and declare, "The Lord God of Israel, He alone is God." This miracle reestablished God's presence and authority.

In the New Testament, we often see the gifts of healings coupled with the working of miracles for much the same reason as in the Old Testament—God revealed Jesus as His Son and established His love and compassion for us by removing the sufferings of mankind. Jesus operated in both the working of miracles to establish His power and authority, and then very predominantly in the gifts of healings, which is why twenty-seven of His recorded miracles involved healing the sick, casting out unclean spirits, and raising the dead.

The working of miracles in the New Testament is seen often in supernatural multiplication, like when Jesus took the little boy's lunch and fed 5,000 men, which means many more were fed when you include women and children (John 6:1-13). Later in the same chapter, Jesus, operating through the working of miracles, altered the laws of nature when He walked on water (John 6:16-20). Other examples in the New Testament include Steven, full of faith and power, who did great wonders and miracles among the people (Acts 6:8). God worked unusual miracles by the hands of Paul so that even handkerchiefs or aprons were brought from his body to the sick, and the diseases left them (Acts 19:11-12).

This miracle could be somewhat confusing based on what I said earlier about healings; however, the actual miracle here was that the laws of nature were altered when he took a common piece of cloth and transferred miracle working power to heal onto them. When the believers carried the cloths back and laid the handkerchief on the sick, they were immediately healed and diseases left them.

My wife Lisa and I did this very thing when we attended an "All Faiths Crusade" in Detroit, Michigan, in the fall of 1998. Dr. Kenneth E. Hagin had asked believers to bring handkerchiefs or clothes to transfer the anointing onto them to carry back to loved ones who could not physically attend the crusade. My grandmother Viola had just gone through open-heart surgery and was very weak. Lisa and I drove from New York to attend the crusade to have our young faith bolstered and to have them anoint a prayer cloth to take back to my grandmother.

As I said, Lisa and I were very young in the Lord, and we saw and learned things while we were there that changed our lives, including the fact that brother Hagin actually called us forward and laid hands on us. We took that prayer cloth back to my grandmother and had her place it over her heart until she totally recovered. My grandmother was a Southern Baptist, and we needed that prayer cloth as a point of contact to help build her faith because she was not taught to believe that God still healed the sick.

My dear friend and brother Gabriel, who is an evangelist on the mission fields in Central America, told me of a miracle he received that altered the laws of nature. Gabriel was walking through the jungle carrying his guitar (without a case) and his Bible when a sudden storm came out of nowhere and began pouring down very heavy rain. Gabriel cried out loudly to the Lord in the storm, "Father, help me! I cannot let my guitar get wet or it will be ruined, and You know I need this guitar to reach the lost!" Immediately right over him a small pocket opened where it was not raining, and as he kept walking, that small pocket stayed right over his head. He could see the rain all around him, but it did not rain on him for the entire rest of his journey!

More than any other time in church history, we need to develop our faith to walk in these supernatural manifestations and demonstrate the genuine power of God to our lost and hopeless generation. Sings and wonders follow the preaching of the word!

Gifts of Healings

The gifts of healings are manifestations of the Holy Spirit in the sphere of disease. As I stated earlier, the working of miracles is a sign that manifests the authority and power of God, and the gifts of healings manifest to heal and are a sign of the mercy and love of God. No doubt there is much that medical science has done to help in the suffering of humanity by natural means; however, the gifts of healings are supernatural and stand alone from any other natural means or circumstance.

The gifts of healings is plural for there are many types of healings that are manifested through the gifts of healings. Howard Carter describes the gifts of healings like a bunch of grapes hanging from a single stalk; just like there are classes of diseases, each of the gifts of healings is like one of the grapes in the bunch that has a counteracting effect on some particular class of disease.

Sickness and disease typically manifests in one or more of these classifications:

- Blood disorders / autoimmune diseases
- Nervous system / neurological disorders
- Body or bone / flesh disorders and diseases
- Demonic / unclean spiritual attacks

A person operating in the gifts of healings may be used by God to heal folks in all these classifications or only one or two specific areas. For example, I was miraculously healed of an autoimmune disease many years ago when I first truly learned what Scripture taught about divine healing. Since that time, my faith has manifested the gifts of healings over and over again through our ministry as Lisa and I have seen countless folks healed from autoimmune disorders including ulcerative colitis, Crohn's disease, IBS, and diverticulitis.

The same is true with my wife, Lisa, who was super-naturally healed of Hashimoto's thyroiditis and Grave's disease, which are autoimmune diseases that affect the thyroid gland. After we stood confidently on God's Word and promises for her healing, she, too, was miraculously healed! Now she preaches with boldness that God is our Healer through the mighty name of Jesus, and continues to see many others recover and receive complete healing from various autoimmune diseases, cancers, and body, bone, and flesh diseases.

Some believers seem to be anointed with one or more gifts (grapes) that specifically manifest with great consistency for miracles in specific areas, like the deaf recovering their hearing, while another may experience great success in causing the blind to recover their sight.

You may be wondering what category cancer fits into. Cancer is caused by a demon, and it can manifest in any of the four classifications listed above. Just as Jesus did with all demonic spirits, you have to cast cancer out and command healing to manifest. Lisa and I have multiple testimonies of those healed from cancer through our ministry. We have also witnessed or heard many testimonies of others who were healed of cancer and other debilitating diseases from the ministries of many great men and women of God whom we associate with or follow.

This is another reason why the gifts of healings is plural, and that's because there are many different supernatural methods God uses to heal the sick. One might anoint with oil, another may press mud into a blind man's eyes, another may lay hands on the sick, another may just command the sick to be healed. In the case of Naaman, it was dipping in a muddy river seven times to be healed of leprosy.

> There are diversities of gifts, but the **same Spirit**. There are differences of ministries, but the **same Lord**. And there are diversities of activities, but it is the **same God** who works all in all. **But the manifestation of the Spirit is given to each one for the profit of all** (1 Corinthians 12:4-7).

The same Holy Spirit who convicts the lost and brings salvation today is the same Holy Spirit who brings healing to the sick today just like He did in days past. The same God who healed all who were sick in the Gospels is the same God who still heals all who are sick today. Too many people stand by and watch their loved ones die needlessly before their time because they have been taught to believe God doesn't heal anymore. God does heal today through the same power of the Holy Spirit that Jesus operated in. The only thing that can stop you from receiving is unbelief.

> Then Jesus told them, "A prophet is honored everywhere except in his own hometown and among his relatives and his own family." And **because of their unbelief**, he couldn't do any miracles among them except to place his hands on a few sick people and heal them. And he was amazed at their unbelief (Mark 6:4-6 NLT).

If unbelief hindered Jesus, it will hinder you too. Don't be a so-called believer in name only and an unbeliever in the power gifts of the Spirit!

The Utterance Gifts

Prophecy

The three gifts that say something are listed in order of importance; prophecy is the most important because it takes the gift of tongues and the gift of interpretation together to equal what prophecy accomplishes. Prophecy brings forth edification, exhortation, and comfort to those who hear it.

> Pursue love, and desire spiritual gifts, **but especially that you may prophesy**. For he who speaks in a tongue does not speak to men but to God, for no one understands him; however,

> in the spirit he speaks mysteries. But he who prophesies speaks **edification** and **exhortation** and **comfort** to men (1 Corinthians 14:1-3).

Prophecy is an utterance in a known language, an inspired utterance that comes forth spontaneously from your spirit rather than your head, and is a supernatural gift of the Spirit meant to grab people's attention. In its purest form, prophecy does not contain revelation; there is no forth-telling or any type of revealing something unknown in a simple prophecy. Its purpose is to build up those who hear it, just like this passage says: for edification, exhortation, and comfort.

When a believer is used to deliver a word of prophecy, this does not mean they are a prophet, for there is much more that would need to be evident in a person's life to be called into the office of a prophet. However, a prophet will often use the gift of prophecy along with one of the revelation gifts such as a word of knowledge or a word of wisdom to reveal specific details the Lord wants known through a prophetic utterance. We discussed the word of wisdom and knowledge earlier, so here we will just talk about the gift of prophecy.

Here is a simple illustration to make this clearer. If someone adds cream and sugar to their coffee, it is still called "coffee," yet in its truest sense, coffee is black without additional ingredients added. It's the same with prophecy; it is meant to edify, comfort, and exhort; however, sometimes revelation gifts might be present along with the prophecy. We should follow what Paul taught concerning the supernatural gift of prophecy and desire that we all speak by inspired utterances in prophecy.

> Therefore, brethren, **desire earnestly to prophesy, and do not forbid to speak with tongues** (1 Corinthians 14:39).

> And when Paul had laid hands on them, the Holy Spirit came upon them, and **they spoke with tongues and prophesied** (Acts 19:6).

Before Paul laid his hands on the believers in Ephesus to receive the Holy Spirit, they said to him, "We have not so much as heard whether there is a Holy Spirit." Not only did they receive the indwelling Holy Spirit and spoke in tongues, but they also received the ability to be used in the gift of prophecy. Even though they had just been filled, they were able to operate in other gifts because it is not based on stature, but on simple faith alone as Holy Spirit wills.

King David prophesied when he uttered the Psalms. He prophesied about the goodness of God and how He takes care of His own, which would certainly be encouraging and comforting. David also used prophecy to be predictive with a word of wisdom and spoke of the coming Messiah and about future events for Israel; again, this is like coffee with cream and sugar added.

We can summarize that the gift of prophecy can be used for many purposes by the Holy Spirit in the life of a believer, but it will always remain as inspired utterance in its simplest form.

Different Kinds of Tongues

The gift of different kinds of tongues is not the same as the personal tongues or prayer language each believer receives when they are baptized in the Holy Spirit. When accompanied by the interpretation of tongues, different kinds of tongues is the equivalent to prophecy in that the purpose is to edify, to exhort, and to comfort. Again, in the order of importance, prophecy is the most important, but speaking in tongues is the most prominent. Tongues is the initial evidence that you have received the Holy Spirit, and every believer should be filled with the Holy Spirit after they get saved.

> And they were all filled with the Holy Spirit and began to speak with other tongues, as the Spirit gave them utterance (Acts 2:4).

Speaking in tongues is for building up the believer during times of personal prayer, and when it is accompanied by interpretation it can be used to build up a body of believers. Tongues and interpretation of tongues are gifts that only appear in the New Testament. We can find all of the other seven gifts of the Spirit in operation in the Old Testament, but tongues is only found in the New

Testament because we could not pray in tongues until we received a recreated, born-again spirit.

Tongues is the language of God; it is not initiated in your head, but from your spirit, or as the Bible says, in your belly there are rivers of living water that flow out of you. Jesus told the disciples before He was taken up that there would be specific signs that would follow or manifest in the life of a believer, and tongues was a specific sign.

> And these signs will follow those who believe: In My name they will cast out demons; **they will speak with new tongues**; they will take up serpents; and if they drink anything deadly, it will by no means hurt them; they will lay hands on the sick, and they will recover (Mark 16:17-18).

Just a side note to ponder. When God declared, "Let there be light," what dialect do you think He spoke? There were no men on the earth yet so there was no need for the known languages of man. God speaks His own language, and He allows us to speak His language when we are filled with the Holy Spirit and speak in tongues.

> For **he who speaks in a tongue** does not speak to men but to God, for no one under-stands him; however, **in the spirit he speaks mysteries** (1 Corinthians 14:2).

Tongues is the supernatural language of heaven that allows my spirit to speak directly to God through Holy Spirit. Tongues bypasses my mind and intellect so I speak things that are mysteries to me, and I pray for the perfect will of God to manifest in my life.

> And the Holy Spirit helps us in our weakness. For example, we don't know what God wants us to pray for. **But the Holy Spirit prays for us** with groanings that cannot be expressed in words. And the Father who knows all hearts knows what the Spirit is saying, for **the Spirit pleads for us believers in harmony with God's own will** (Romans 8:26-27 NLT).

Paul instructed every believer to be filled with the Holy Spirit just like he did in Ephesus when he first came across the believers who had not even heard of the Holy Spirit. Later, he wrote these instructions to the church in Ephesus:

> Don't be drunk with wine, because that will ruin your life. Instead, **be filled with the Holy Spirit**, singing psalms and hymns and spiritual songs among yourselves, and making music to the Lord in your hearts (Ephesians 5:18-19 NLT).

Some Greek translations suggest that "be filled" literally should be translated as the phase "be being filled." We should continually look to receive a fresh infilling, and that is exactly what praying in tongues does for the individual believer. It is building up or super-charging our faith and spirit.

As a believer, there may be times while in a church service when you receive by inspiration of the Holy Spirit a message to be released through the gift of different kinds tongues. If this happens, it must be accompanied by the gift of interpretation so that the whole church can be built up. These two gifts operating together in a corporate setting become a sign to unbelievers that the power of God is present.

> Therefore **tongues are for a sign, not to those who believe but to unbelievers**; but prophesying is not for unbelievers but for those who believe (1 Corinthians 14:22).

Not everyone will be used to give a message through the gift of tongues, but every believer should be and needs to be baptized with the Holy Spirit and fire with the evidence of speaking in tongues.

This difference between the gift of tongues we just covered and the personal tongues of every believer is what confused my friend in the car that night that I spoke of in Chapter 4 when he asked, "If tongues are still for today, then why does it say in the Bible, 'Do all have the ability to speak in tongues?'" I did not know until I went to Bible college that there was a difference, and I hope I have also made it plain for you to now know the difference as well.

Interpretation of Tongues

The gift of interpretation of tongues has both a min-istry function as well as a persnal interpretation function. It is the least of all the nine gifts because it is depen-dent on the gift of different kinds of tongues in order to operate. Sometimes after praying in tongues, a believer may also begin to pray in their understanding with an unction directed by the Holy Spirit and interpret your own tongues.

> Therefore let him who speaks in a tongue pray that he may interpret. For if I pray in a tongue, my spirit prays, but my understanding is unfruitful (1 Corinthians 14:13-14).

An *unction* is something we cannot generate on our own. It is holy and powerful; it's an overwhelming ener-gizing push forward from the Holy Spirit. It is difficult to explain, but I will give you an example of when this has happened to me.

My pastor was preaching the gospel in a foreign country that was somewhat dangerous to be in, and I had committed to pray for him while he was gone. I was interceding for him and those who were with him and I began to pray in tongues. After a few moments my tongues changed and became very authoritative in nature. As this continued a while, I began to repeat the same phase in tongues five times or six times. Suddenly, with that same authority and power, I began to interpret my tongues.

I heard myself speaking a series of protective declarations that all began with the phrase, "Satan, I forbid you not," and then covered several specific areas as the Lord gave me the utterance—from creating strife and chaos that would disrupt their meetings, to disrupting the flow of their finances, provisions, and favor, and so on with the other strongly worded declarations that would forbid Satan from moving against my pastor and his team.

I have interpreted my own tongues on other notable occasions as well; however, on most of those occasions I did not know ahead of time that it was about to happen until the gift rose up in me and I released the interpretation. We don't have to understand what we are saying every time we are praying in tongues; though it's a mystery to us, it's not to God. I have heard it said that sometimes if we knew the things we were praying in the spirit we might not pray them out at all.

> For he who speaks in a tongue does not speak to men but to God, for no one understands him; however, **in the spirit he speaks mysteries** (1 Corinthians 14:2).

I have also been in church services and after someone has stood up and delivered a message in tongues, I knew I had the interpretation. Sometimes I stood and said, "I have the interpretation." Other times, I held my peace while another person gave the interpretation. It's an amazing spiritual moment when the interpretation someone else gives lines up exactly with what you received—it is a powerful God-confirmation moment!

One last thing to know about the gift of interpretation is that it is not a translation. When an interpretation follows a message given in tongues, you are not *translating* the message but *interpreting* the message because Holy Spirit wants it conveyed in a known language. The gift of interpretation, as with all the gifts, is meant to help believers be equipped and grow in their faith. Anyone can be used by the Holy Spirit to interpret a tongue.

Here are just a few well-known, time-tested, trusted sources to study about the gifts of the Spirit and how they flow. I gleaned information from all four of these books that are in my personal library.

- *The Holy Spirit and His Gifts* by Kenneth E. Hagin
- *Questions and Answers on Spiritual Gifts* by Howard Cater
- *Smith Wigglesworth on Spiritual Gifts* by Smith Wigglesworth
- *The Gifts and Ministries of the Holy Spirit* by Lester Sumrall
- *Flowing in the Holy Spirit* by Rodney Howard-Browne

We need to learn how to flow in the gifts, and along with studying and reading all you can from trusted sources, it is imperative to attend services where the Holy Spirit is moving through believers.

Faith Declaration

Father, I believe You are the God of miracles, signs, and wonders, and I desire the gifts of the Spirit to work through me. Use me to glorify the Lord Jesus in my life. Oh, that I may be "being filled" over and over again with Holy Spirit so that out of my innermost being will flow rivers of living water. Use me, Lord, to manifest Your presence and power to my generation!

Chapter 7: Receive the Holy Spirit

While Apollos was in Corinth, Paul traveled through the interior regions until he reached Ephesus, on the coast, where he found several believers. **"Did you receive the Holy Spirit when you believed?" he asked them. "No," they replied, "we haven't even heard that there is a Holy Spirit."** (Acts 19:1-2 NLT).

On his third missionary journey, Paul set out to preach and teach the salvation message of redemption through Jesus. After he left Corinth, Paul traveled to Ephesus. There Paul met some believers and after talking with them, he asked them if they had received the Holy Spirit since they believed. Their response was very telling: "We haven't even heard that there is a Holy Spirit." As a young Bible school student, this scripture captured my heart, and I knew teaching people who they are in Christ and about the Holy Spirit would always be a large part of our ministry.

Let's look at what Paul did with these believers in Ephesus. First, Paul asked them what baptism they received. They responded, "The baptism of John unto repentance." Paul immediately pointed them to Jesus, the one who would come after John, and they were baptized in the name of Jesus. Once they received salvation and were baptized in the name of Jesus, Paul laid his hands on them and they received the Holy Spirit and began to speak in tongues and prophesy.

> While Apollos was in Corinth, Paul traveled through the interior regions until he reached Ephesus, on the coast, where he found several believers. **"Did you receive the Holy Spirit when you believed?" he asked them. "No," they replied, "we haven't even heard that there is a Holy Spirit."** "Then what baptism did you experience?" he asked. And they replied, "The baptism of John." Paul said, "John's baptism called for repentance from sin. But John himself told the people to believe in the one who would come later, meaning Jesus." As soon as they heard this, they were baptized in the name of the Lord Jesus. **Then when Paul laid his hands on them, the Holy Spirit came on them, and they spoke in other tongues and prophesied** (Acts 19:1-6 NLT).

When I became born again on March 18, 1984, I was by myself in my barracks room on Wright Patterson Air

Force Base in Fairborn, Ohio. I was radically saved that morning; you can read my full testimony in my book *Consider the Squirrel*. However, I did not get filled with the Holy Spirit with the evidence in speaking in tongues until thirteen days later in Saratoga Springs, New York.

I had a very basic Southern Baptist understanding of why I needed to be born again, and I did not have any understanding of the ministry of Holy Spirit or His gifts. In fact, until I was baptized in the Holy Ghost and experienced the power of the Holy Spirit for myself, all I ever heard about praying in tongues was negative and denominational gibberish.

That afternoon in Saratoga Springs, after a short teaching about being filled with the Holy Spirit, the believers I was with laid hands on me to receive the baptism and fire. I prayed a very simple prayer as they gathered around me. I had my face covered with my hands and I prayed, "Father, if You in heaven saved me, and if You want me here on the earth to have Your power, then fill me." With that, I immediately began to speak in other tongues.

It really was that simple! All I had to do was receive and act in faith. By saying, "act in faith," what I mean is that I had to open my mouth and allow the divine utterance of the Lord to come out of my mouth. I didn't care how foolish it sounded or whether it was fluent or not.

I began to speak in tongues, albeit somewhat apprehensively at first, but no less by faith, and it pleased God.

We had a two-and-a-half-hour ride home that evening back to the military base where we were all stationed, and I prayed quietly in tongues the whole ride home. That was March 31, 1984, and I have been cooperating with Holy Spirit ever since. We will never exhaust His wisdom or power.

My wife, Lisa, also has an extraordinary testimony of her own salvation and how she received the baptism of the Holy Spirit. On Wednesday night, April 13, 1983, Lisa went to church with her sister to an Assemblies of God church in Rome, New York. The speaker that night was a Catholic nun who took the pulpit and began immediately praying in tongues. Lisa said she prayed in tongues so long that Lisa began to shake. All she could think was, *Would you please just stop so I can run up front and get saved?*

The power of the Holy Spirit was so evident through the gift of tongues on that little Catholic nun that nothing more was needed for folks to come to the altar and get saved that night. A short time later, one night as Lisa was kneeling at the side of her bed praying for more of the Holy Spirit in her life, she began to pray in tongues. She received just what she was asking for with simple faith. She shifted over from praying in her known language to praying in her heavenly language and began building herself up.

> But you, beloved, building yourselves up
> on your most holy faith, praying in the

Holy Spirit, keep yourselves in the love of God, looking for the mercy of our Lord Jesus Christ unto eternal life (Jude 1:20-21).

Receiving the Holy Spirit is not a difficult task, it is as simple as receiving salvation. The same Holy Spirit who helped you become born again in Jesus' name is the same Holy Spirit who will baptize you with power and who prays with you in tongues.

And the Holy Spirit helps us in our weakness. For example, we don't know what God wants us to pray for. **But the Holy Spirit prays for us with groanings that cannot be expressed in words**. And the Father who knows all hearts knows what the Spirit is saying, for **the Spirit pleads for us believers in harmony with God's own will**. And we know that God causes everything to work together for the good of those who love God and are called according to his purpose for them (Romans 8:26-28 NLT).

Once you are filled with the Holy Spirit with the evidence of speaking in tongues, find a solid church that preaches that the Holy Spirit is still active in the lives of believers today, just as He was in the book of Acts for the early believers. Desire the gifts of the Spirit to work in your life and return to your first love. Do you remember what it was like when you first got saved and believed

God could do anything? He hasn't changed, so quit listening to naysayers and unbelieving church folk.

Become insatiably hungry for the things of God. Just like a mechanic invests in the tools of his trade, you should invest in the kingdom. Read your Bible, pray, read books about the miracles of God, sow into the work of the ministry with your time, talents, and finances, watch videos and listen to podcasts that celebrate the power of God, and grow your relationship with Him.

Stay in fellowship with other strong believers, become a soul winner, and work to see others saved and filled with the same power you have received. Preach the good news to everyone and ask God for strategies to reach the lost, especially your own family. Know that He will work with you and confirm His Word with signs and wonders. Expect to see miracles working through your life, be convinced that all things are possible, and live in perpetual Pentecost by being constantly filled and by keeping your faith built up.

Refuse to allow others to put out your fire with their unbelief; refuse to become a lukewarm, diluted believer; burn white hot for God with His promise that you can do the same and greater works than what Jesus did during His earthly ministry. This is exactly what Jesus wants for all believers who pray in His name and believe in the power of the Holy Spirit.

Cast out devils, speak in new tongues, lead the lost to Christ, lay hands on the sick so they can recover, and know this: the Lord will work with you and through you with accompanying signs and wonders.

> And He said to them, "Go into all the world and preach the gospel to every creature. He who believes and is baptized will be saved; but he who does not believe will be condemned. And these signs will follow those who believe: In My name they will cast out demons; they will speak with new tongues; they will take up serpents; and if they drink anything deadly, it will by no means hurt them; they will lay hands on the sick, and they will recover." So then, after the Lord had spoken to them, He was received up into heaven, and sat down at the right hand of God. And they went out and preached everywhere, the Lord working with *them* and confirming the word through the accompanying signs. Amen (Mark 16:15-20).

Faith Declaration

> *Lord Jesus, I desire the best gifts of the Spirit to operate in my life, I ask You now to fill me with Your Spirit and baptize with the Holy Spirit and fire with the evidence of speaking in tongues, in Jesus' name!*

Other Books by the Author

**Consider the Squirrel:
A Collection of Modern-Day Parables**

ISBN: 979-8-9927288-0-4

People have attempted to define God and themselves through religion, but religion is only a human attempt to encounter God on our own terms. Religion is boring; it has been unable to capture the heart and imagination of who God is. The Bible has plenty to say about who He is, who man is, and how we can live our lives with passion, purpose, and fulfillment. This is what Bobby Coleman brings to light. Laying hold of the truths with-in this book will help you discover the limitless expanse of who God is and how He functions in order to benefit your life. It is time to Consider the Squirrel!

Look for *Consider the Squirrel* by Bobby Coleman wherever you buy books Online!

About the Author

Bobby and Lisa Coleman pastor the River Gainesville Church in Florida and are the co-founders of Open Skies Ministries. They are currently acquiring land for their new ministry base, the Open Skies Ranch.

The ranch will serve as a place to refresh and train believers for revival. It will host ministers and their families, conferences for men, women, and married couples, youth and children's summer camps, and specialized ministry for veterans and first responders.

The heart of their ministry is to win the lost and to see believers baptized in the Holy Spirit and fire making disciples who will fulfill the great commission as they go into all the world.

For more information about their ministry or to schedule revival meetings with Bobby and Lisa Coleman, please e-mail:

rivergainesvillechurch@gmail.com

or visit:
Website: www.rivergainesville.com
Facebook: River Gainesville